Southern
African

LBJs

made simple

Doug Newman
Gordon King

This book is dedicated to Mike King for his depth of knowledge
and training in data methodology techniques, without which the
logic of this book would never have happened.

AUTHORS' ACKNOWLEDGEMENTS
Special thanks to Pippa Parker, without whose belief in and understanding of our vision this book would not have been possible; also to Colette Alves and Dominic Robson for their expertise in editing and design. Thanks to Geoff Lockwood for his invaluable input and advice throughout the project. In addition we thank Sarah Garner, Karen Fick, Joan King and Mike King for believing. We thank the following for their contributions: Norman Arlott, Patrik Åberg, Tamar Cassidy, Marcell Claassen, Callan Cohen, Jeff da Costa, Eric Ehlers, Neil Gray, Clem Haagner, Ron Jackson, Peter Kaestner, Linda Macaulay, Brian McCormick, Mike Nelson, Niall Perrins, Gary Preskil, Peter Ryan, Ian Sinclair, Derek Solomon, Tony Usher, and Tamar Cassidy of the Ditsong National Museum of Natural History.

Published by Struik Nature
(an imprint of Penguin Random House
South Africa (Pty) Ltd)
Reg. No. 1953/000441/07
The Estuaries No. 4, Oxbow Crescent, Century
Avenue, Century City, 7441
PO Box 1144, Cape Town, 8000, South Africa

Visit www.penguinrandomhouse.co.za and join
the Struik Nature Club for updates, news, events
and special offers.

First published in 2011
Second edition 2021

10 9 8 7 6 5 4 3 2 1

Copyright © in text, 2011, 2021: Doug Newman &
Gordon King
Copyright © in photographs, 2011, 2021: Doug Newman
or as listed above
Copyright © in published edition, 2011, 2021:
Penguin Random House South Africa (Pty) Ltd

Publisher: Pippa Parker
Managing editor: Roelien Theron
Editor: Colette Alves
Designer: Dominic Robson
Proofreader: Thea Grobbelaar

Reproduction by Studio Repro
Printed and bound in China by RR Donnelley

MIX
Paper from
responsible sources
FSC
www.fsc.org
FSC® C144853

ISBN 978 1 77584 653 6 (Print)
ISBN 978 1 77584 659 8 (ePub)

STRUIK NATURE CALL APP

DOWNLOAD FREE APP
to access the calls in this book by scanning
a QR code or visiting the relevant app store.

See page 9 for further information
on the call app.

Apple App Store

Google Play Store

Contents

INTRODUCTION

This book is quite unlike a normal field guide in that it has been written specifically to address the difficult problem of identifying LBJs (Little Brown Jobs) in the field. In it we present a methodology that, if followed scrupulously, will guide you to the correct identification of the LBJ in question. The process is cumulative, building on information gleaned at each of three stages: the reader will confront the characteristics first of the LBJ **family**, then of the relevant **visual group** within that family, and finally the **key pointers** that distinguish the **species**, which are only relevant within that blue visual group. The sum total of family, visual group and species pointers will result in a positive identification at species level.

It is therefore essential to work through the introduction, especially 'How to use this book', and follow each step that will lead you to the correct identification. If you simply flick through the book hoping to find your mystery LBJ, you are unlikely to make a positive identification and will probably become more confused than ever. Gradually, with repeated use of the book's system, you will acquire both confidence and a better knowledge of families and visual groups, and you will have advanced a long way towards conquering the challenges posed by LBJs.

As an example, simply paging through the book to Eastern Long-billed Lark (page 75) will give you the pointers 'long tail', 'habitat' and 'distribution', which in isolation are not helpful to identify the species. If, however, you start at the front of the book and separate first the families (page 12), then the visual groups within the lark family (page 61) and finally arrive at Eastern Long-billed Lark, the cumulative pointers will be:

Family (PURPLE):	- robust build - bill heavier than in pipits - does not 'wag' tail - most species ground-based - forages by walking slowly and deliberately (compare pipits) - usually solitary or in pairs (sparrow-larks in small flocks)
Visual group (BLUE):	- long, decurved bill
Species (ORANGE/RED):	- long tail - habitat - distribution

This cumulative system gives you 10 pointers for Eastern Long-billed Lark.

NOTE: Because this book focuses on the identification of LBJs, not all species in a family group are necessarily included. Where species are fairly simple to identify, such as in some of the flycatchers, they have been omitted from this book.

BIRDING TIPS

When you're out in the field trying to identify a bird, observe it closely for some time before drawing any conclusions as to its identity. A quick glance is unlikely to reveal anything about its behaviour and may not even give you enough opportunity to note correctly its physical characteristics and relative size.

Size

Discerning the relative size of a bird is a skill that develops with time and field experience. Remember that when you're using binoculars, a bird at a distance in your field of view often appears larger than one that is close. When you're looking at a bird, it is often helpful to compare its size to that of another species you know well.

Sedge Warbler
(13 cm)

Eastern Clapper Lark
(15 cm)

Cape Longclaw
(20 cm)

Coloration

The colour and markings of birds can vary within a species, so it is advisable to view an illustration of, say, a Tawny-flanked Prinia as a **general** rather than an 'absolute' representation of that species. The bird you are looking at may, for example, appear to have a larger rufous wing panel than is shown in the corresponding illustration, but this is relevant only if the size of the rufous wing panel (rather than its presence) is listed as an identifying characteristic.

Bear in mind that feathers age, so pale edges can become worn and bold colours will appear bleached. This is particularly important just before birds moult at the end of summer and winter, when plumages are at their oldest and most worn. At these times, the colour pointers that you are looking for may be more difficult to discern.

Tawny-flanked Prinia

Light and weather conditions

Light is crucial when you are attempting to identify a bird as colours often appear different, depending on the prevailing light. This is particularly noticeable for the bill and legs: when a bird is between you and the sun, light can illuminate the blood flow in the legs and bill, making them seem more pink than usual. In cloudy conditions, or if the bird is in the shade, plumage coloration often appears richer than when the bird is in full sun.

Bright, direct sunlight

Deep shade

Photography

Digital cameras have become an invaluable tool in bird ID, enabling you to take a photograph of the mystery bird and identify it later. They do, however, have limitations. Cameras are susceptible to a phenomenon known as 'white balance', which may render the subject more red or blue, making it very difficult to judge the true colour. Furthermore, in both digital and film photography, chromatic aberration, or colour fringing, can add subtle red or blue fringes to the edge of the subject, potentially causing colours to change.

Perhaps the most limiting factor of photography is that it is very difficult to judge a bird's size and jizz from a picture. It is often best to take several photos of the bird from different angles and distances, as well as another species, if possible, to provide a benchmark for size. It is almost impossible to see behaviour from a static image, but you can remind yourself of the bird's habitat by taking photos of the surroundings in which you found it.

Behaviour

As in other animals, a bird's behaviour depends on the situation and will not necessarily reflect the traits you expect when you first see it. This is particularly true of pipits, for example. If you have just flushed a pipit from the grass, it will be difficult to observe its feeding style and characteristic tail-wagging behaviour until it has had a chance to settle down. Thus, it is important to observe quietly and allow the bird to calm down and get used to your presence. It will soon revert to its normal behaviour. Playing recorded calls often alarms a bird, causing it to behave in an unusual manner.

Observe quietly and allow the bird to calm down and get used to your presence.

BIRDING BY EAR

A bird's call is an important element in birding. First, it often serves as a means of locating a bird long before you see it. Secondly – and this is particularly valuable in the case of similar-looking species such as LBJs – the call, songs in particular, can be a crucial aid to identification. It is worth noting that many species have very similar alarm calls. As you work through the calls in the book (see 'How to use this book' on page 8 for information on using the call barcodes), you will notice how important it is to develop an ear for bird calls.

Don't be disheartened if it takes you a while to get the hang of separating similar-sounding calls. You may think you are unable to bird by ear, but if you can recognise a person's voice without seeing them, you are already able to hear and understand the most important vocal qualities: pitch, tone, inflection and phrasing. The human brain cannot process all the external stimuli it receives, and it develops filters in order to absorb what is important. That is why, for example, in a room full of people all talking at once, if someone says your name you will pick it out. These filters take time to develop and they constantly change as you practise your listening skills. It can take a year or more to be able to hear the subtle differences between warbler calls, for instance. Comparative tracks will help you get to grips with differences such as these.

Even if you are familiar with the call of a particular species, remember that some species regularly mimic the calls of others. Listen for a while, as a mimic will soon switch to copying another species and thus betray itself as an impostor.

Left: *In dense bush or forest the call often serves as a means of locating a bird.*
Above: *The call of the Rufous-naped Lark is distinctive and a key 'pointer' in identifying this species in the field.*

HOW TO USE THIS BOOK

To isolate one species from a large group of similar-looking birds can be a daunting challenge, but it is made easier if the group is made progressively smaller. In this book we have divided LBJs in southern Africa into 13 'family' groups (and allied species); 'families' in this book broadly follow taxonomic groups, with some exceptions. For accurate taxonomic groups, see the Appendix on page 148. For our purposes, families have been grouped based on appearance, as follows: honeyguides & honeybirds; true warblers & allied species; cisticolas; prinias & prinia-like warblers; larks & sparrow-larks; flycatchers; scrub robins; chats & wheatears; weavers; bishops & allied species; sparrows; pipits & longclaws; and canaries & allied species.

The majority of these groups have been further divided into groups that have easily observable common characteristics. Most of these so-called 'visual groups' contain fewer than 10 species for simplicity.

There are three basic steps to identifying your mystery LBJ:

STEP ONE: separating families

To decide which family group you are dealing with, refer to pages 10–16 and study the illustrations and family features denoted by pointers and in the accompanying text. Once you have found the family group to which your bird belongs, continue to the relevant page as indicated.

Visual pointers for the family

The 'Look for' box summarises important features for the family

Overall family summary

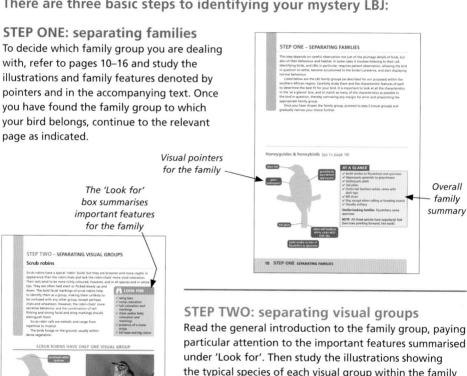

STEP TWO: separating visual groups

Read the general introduction to the family group, paying particular attention to the important features summarised under 'Look for'. Then study the illustrations showing the typical species of each visual group within the family group: the blue pointers show the features that identify each visual group. When you have identified the visual group that includes your bird, turn to the page on which the species accounts for that visual group start.

Blue pointers will help you place your bird in a visual group

STEP THREE: identifying species

Check each species in the visual group. Pointers on each illustration show the characteristic features of that particular species, separating it from others within the same visual group. The characteristic features are repeated in the 'At a glance' block, which summarises not only the visual clues but also other criteria that are important for the species, such as call, distribution and habitat. **A successful identification depends on matching** ALL THREE **features in** orange **type or** ONE **feature in** red **type.** In instances where a red feature is given in addition to three orange features (for example, 'call'), it may be regarded as an alternative matching characteristic. Sometimes two red features are given, in which case these too are alternative matching characteristics.

Similar-looking or -sounding species as well as additional notes are given for ease of reference and comparison.

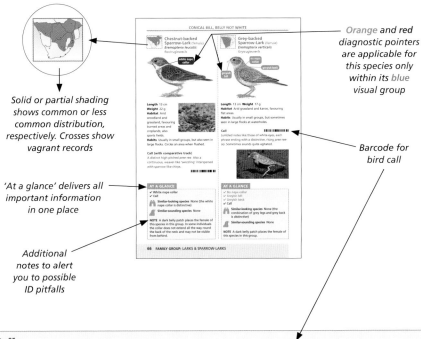

Solid or partial shading shows common or less common distribution, respectively. Crosses show vagrant records

Orange and red diagnostic pointers are applicable for this species only within its blue visual group

'At a glance' delivers all important information in one place

Barcode for bird call

Additional notes to alert you to possible ID pitfalls

Calls

Bird calls and comparative tracks can be accessed by using the free Struik Nature Call App to scan the barcodes. The app can be downloaded onto a smartphone or tablet from Google Play (minimum Android v5.0*) or Apple App Store (minimum iOS 11.4*), by either searching for the app in the app store or using the QR codes on page 2.

To use the app, launch it on your device, then hover the camera over the barcode in the book. The barcode will scan and bring up the call and, where applicable, comparative track for that species. Press 'play' to listen. Internet connectivity is not required to access the calls, as all are contained within the app.

* Minimum operating systems correct at time of printing. Operating systems are updated annually and minimum system requirements will change accordingly.

STEP ONE – SEPARATING FAMILIES

This step depends on careful observation not just of the plumage details of birds, but also of their behaviour and habitat. In some cases it involves listening to their call. Identifying birds, and LBJs in particular, requires patient observation, allowing the bird in question to settle, become accustomed to the birder's presence, and start displaying normal behaviour.

Listed below are the LBJ family groups (as described for our purposes) within the southern African region. Carefully study them and the characteristic features of each to determine the best fit for your bird. It is important to look at all the characteristics in the 'at a glance' box, and to match as many of the characteristics as possible to the bird in question, thereby narrowing any margin for error and pinpointing the appropriate family group.

Once you have chosen the family group, proceed to step 2 (visual groups) and gradually narrow your choice further.

Honeyguides & honeybirds (go to page 18)

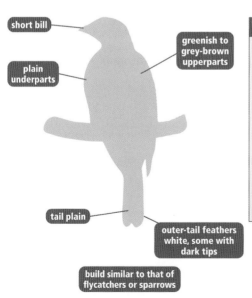

short bill

plain underparts

greenish to grey-brown upperparts

tail plain

outer-tail feathers white, some with dark tips

build similar to that of flycatchers or sparrows

AT A GLANCE

✔ Build similar to flycatchers and sparrows
✔ Upperparts greenish to grey-brown
✔ Underparts plain
✔ Tail plain
✔ Outer-tail feathers white, some with dark tips
✔ Bill short
✔ Shy, except when calling or hawking insects
✔ Usually solitary

Similar-looking families Flycatchers; some sparrows

NOTE All these species have zygodactyl feet (two toes pointing forward, two back).

True warblers & allied species (go to page 22)

Common Whitethroat, Thrush Nightingale, warblers (excluding cisticola-like and prinia-like warblers), rush-, reed-, swamp- and marsh-warblers

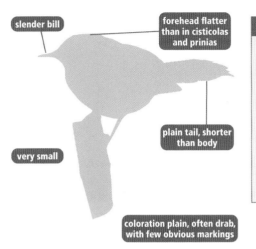

slender bill

forehead flatter than in cisticolas and prinias

plain tail, shorter than body

very small

coloration plain, often drab, with few obvious markings

AT A GLANCE

✔ Very small
✔ Coloration plain, often drab, with few obvious markings
✔ Forehead flatter than in cisticolas and prinias
✔ Slender bill
✔ Plain tail, shorter than body
✔ Occurs in dense cover (trees, bushes and reed beds)
✔ Usually solitary, but territories quite small

Similar-looking families Plain cisticolas; prinias

Cisticolas (go to page 36)

head rounder than in true warblers

back usually with bold markings (but sometimes plain)

strong bill

very small

coloration rich brown

AT A GLANCE

✔ Very small
✔ Coloration rich brown
✔ Back usually with bold markings (but sometimes plain)
✔ Head rounder than in true warblers
✔ Strong bill
✔ Tail length varies from short to long
✔ Perches prominently or performs aerial displays
✔ Usually solitary or in pairs; family groups when breeding

Similar-looking families Plain cisticolas are like prinias and some warblers.

NOTE Lazy Cisticola is the only cisticola that cocks its tail.

Prinias & prinia-like warblers (go to page 57)

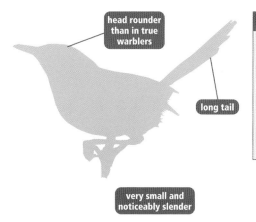

head rounder than in true warblers

long tail

very small and noticeably slender

AT A GLANCE

✔ Very small and noticeably slender
✔ Head rounder than in true warblers
✔ Long tail
✔ Flicks tail persistently
✔ Calls from a prominent perch
✔ Darts very energetically between bushes
✔ Solitary or in pairs or small groups

Similar-looking families Warblers; plain cisticolas

Larks & sparrow-larks (go to page 61)

does not 'wag' tail

bill heavier than in pipits

shorter legs with tibia shorter than in pipits

robust build

AT A GLANCE

✔ Robust build
✔ Bill heavier than in pipits
✔ Shorter legs with tibia shorter than in pipits
✔ Does not 'wag' tail
✔ Most species ground-based except when calling
✔ Forages by walking slowly and deliberately (compare pipits)
✔ Usually solitary or in pairs; sparrow-larks usually in small flocks

Similar-looking families Fine-billed species resemble pipits; conical-billed species are like some female/non-breeding male bishops, indigobirds and whydahs.

Flycatchers (go to page 87)

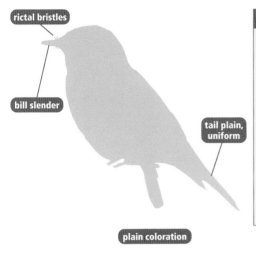

rictal bristles

bill slender

tail plain, uniform

plain coloration

AT A GLANCE

✔ Plain coloration
✔ Tail plain, uniform
✔ Bill slender
✔ Rictal bristles (at base of bill)
✔ Hawks insects – or drops onto them – from a perch
✔ Usually solitary or in pairs

Similar-looking families Some honeybirds; some chats, but habitats and habits differ

NOTE All flycatchers described here have plain tails. Fiscal Flycatcher and Grey Tit-Flycatcher have white on the outer tail, but these species are too distinctive to be considered LBJs.

Scrub robins (go to page 91)

prominent eyebrow

tail with white tips

robin-like build

AT A GLANCE

✔ Robin-like build
✔ Prominent eyebrow
✔ Tail with white tips
✔ Forages mainly on the ground
✔ Calls very musical, given from a concealed location
✔ Usually solitary or in pairs

Similar-looking families Plain species resemble chats or flycatchers, but the white tail tips are distinctive.

Chats & wheatears (go to page 95)

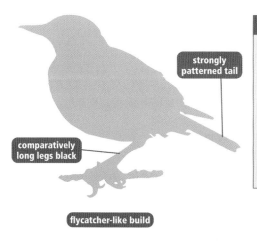

strongly patterned tail

comparatively long legs black

flycatcher-like build

AT A GLANCE

✔ Flycatcher-like build
✔ Strongly patterned tail
✔ Comparatively long legs black
✔ Characteristic wing flicking (chats) or tail wagging (wheatears)
✔ Perches in the open with an upright stance
✔ Usually solitary or in pairs

Similar-looking families Flycatchers and plain scrub robins, but patterned tail, habitat and behaviour are distinctive; some may resemble pipits, but black legs separate them

Weavers (females & non-breeding males) (go to page 103)

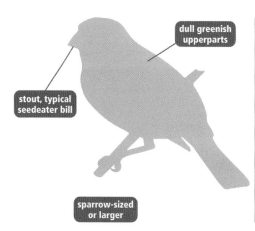

dull greenish upperparts

stout, typical seedeater bill

sparrow-sized or larger

AT A GLANCE

✔ Sparrow-sized or larger
✔ Dull greenish upperparts
✔ Stout, typical seedeater bill
✔ Hops when foraging
✔ Usually in large flocks, often with other seedeaters

Similar-looking families Greenish coloration is distinctive, but browner females may resemble female bishops.

NOTE The breeding male weaver is not always present to give a clue to the identification of the female, so it is important to become familiar with this group.

Bishops & allied species (females & non-breeding males) (go to page 109)

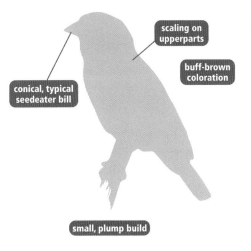

scaling on upperparts

buff-brown coloration

conical, typical seedeater bill

small, plump build

AT A GLANCE

✔ Small, plump build
✔ Buff-brown coloration
✔ Scaling on upperparts
✔ Conical, typical seedeater bill
✔ Hops when foraging
✔ Often in large flocks

Similar-looking families Female/non-breeding male indigobirds and whydahs may resemble some larks; browner weavers, although their build and shades of olive-green tend to make weavers a distinctive family

Sparrows (go to page 125)

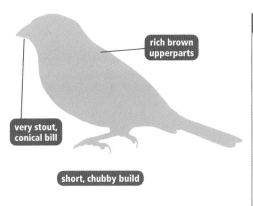

rich brown upperparts

very stout, conical bill

short, chubby build

AT A GLANCE

✔ Short, chubby build
✔ Rich brown upperparts
✔ Very stout, conical bill
✔ Hops when foraging (except Yellow-throated Petronia, which walks)
✔ Occurs in pairs or small flocks

Similar-looking families Some honeybirds; buff-coloured species resemble some female/non-breeding male bishops, but overall the richly coloured upperparts are distinctive.

NOTE Yellow-throated Petronia may be confused with White-browed Sparrow-Weaver or Streaky-headed Seedeater.

Pipits & longclaws (go to page 129)

bill pointed, more slender than in larks

longer legs with tibia longer than in larks

many species 'wag' tail

AT A GLANCE

✔ Bill pointed, more slender than in larks
✔ Longer legs with tibia longer than in larks
✔ Many species 'wag' tail
✔ Most species ground-based
✔ Darts and runs when foraging (compare larks)
✔ Usually solitary or in pairs; sometimes in small flocks
✔ Pinkish legs

Similar-looking families Some larks, but foraging behaviour and 'tail wagging' are distinctive; may resemble some wheatears, but pinkish legs separate.

Canaries & allied species (go to page 140)

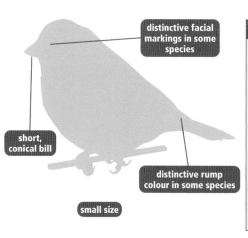

distinctive facial markings in some species

short, conical bill

distinctive rump colour in some species

small size

AT A GLANCE

✔ Small size
✔ Short, conical bill
✔ Distinctive facial markings in some species
✔ Distinctive rump colour in some species
✔ Melodious song
✔ Very seldom ground-based
✔ Often forages on seeding grass stems
✔ Solitary in winter, otherwise in pairs or small flocks; mixes with other seedeaters

Similar-looking families Plain species may resemble some sparrows; brown species may be similar to small female/non-breeding male bishops; Lark-like Bunting may be confused with some larks.

Lesser Swamp Warbler

STEP TWO – SEPARATING VISUAL GROUPS
Honeyguides & honeybirds

For this family, there are two visual groups. The honeyguides and honeybirds are separated mainly on bill structure, with honeyguides having substantially heavier bills than honeybirds.

Both groups are reminiscent of flycatchers or sparrows and are also similar in size to, or slightly larger than (particularly in the case of the Greater Honeyguide), the latter. Their plumage is plain – mainly olive, grey or brownish – but all species have white outer-tail feathers with dark tips. The bills are short, but range from thinnish to stout. The feet are zygodactyl (two toes pointing forward and two back).

Honeyguide calls are usually simple and tend to be repetitive. In some species, individual males call from a specific perch to attract a mate, and will use the same perch over a period of many years.

The birds are mostly sedentary, but show some localised movement in winter. They forage almost exclusively in trees in woodland or forest habitat, where they may be seen hawking insects as flycatchers do (the white outer-tail feathers will identify them as honeyguides).

All honeyguides and honeybirds are brood parasites, laying their eggs in the nests of woodpeckers, barbets, kingfishers, bee-eaters, starlings, flycatchers and cisticolas. As such, they are usually seen alone, except when pairs come together to mate or parasitise a nest. In the latter case, the male may help to distract the host while the female lays the eggs.

> **LOOK FOR**
> ✔ upperpart and underpart coloration
> ✔ chest and/or throat markings
> ✔ bill size and shape
> ✔ size

HONEYGUIDES & HONEYBIRDS CAN BE DIVIDED INTO TWO VISUAL GROUPS

Stout bill (page 19)

Slender bill (page 21)

Greater Honeyguide
(female)
Indicator indicator
Grootheuningwyser

brownish-grey back

Length 20 cm **Weight** 50 g
Habitat Varied (savanna, woodland, grassland). May be found in well-treed gardens.
Habits Normally located when calling or 'guiding', as it perches in an obvious location to attract attention. Attempts to guide humans to beehives.

Call |||||||||||||||||||||| ||| |||
Very distinctive *whit-purrrr* repeated many times from a call site. Also an agitated, squeaky, toy-like chirp as an alarm call.

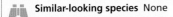
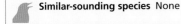
AT A GLANCE

✔ Brownish-grey back
✔ Call

Similar-looking species None

Similar-sounding species None

NOTE The juvenile is similar to the female, but has a dark cap and yellow underparts.

Scaly-throated Honeyguide
Indicator variegatus
Gevlekte Heuningwyser

mottled grey head

olive-green wash to back

heavily mottled chest

Length 19 cm **Weight** 48 g
Habitat Coastal, riverine and montane forest, bushveld and miombo woodland.
Habits Solitary or in pairs. Usually located when the male gives his characteristic call from a perch.

Call ||||||||||||||||| ||| | |||
A shrill, rising screech similar to that of a Barn Owl.

AT A GLANCE

✔ Olive-green wash to back
✔ Heavily mottled chest
✔ Mottled grey head
✔ Call

Similar-looking species None (heavy mottling on chest is distinctive)

Similar-sounding species None

Lesser Honeyguide
Indicator minor
Kleinheuningwyser

plain grey head

olive-green wash to back

plain greyish chest

Length 15 cm
Weight 28 g
Habitat Savanna, woodland and forest, including gardens.
Habits Usually solitary. Often located by the male calling from a perch. Does not guide humans or animals to beehives.

Call (with comparative track)
A very distinctive, double-syllabic *teeu-cheu-cheu-cheu...* (unlike the monosyllabic *tink-tink-tink* of Zitting Cisticola and *tik-tik-tik-tik* of Pallid Honeyguide, which also omits the lead-in *teeu*).

Pallid Honeyguide
Indicator meliphilus
Oostelike Heuningwyser

plain greenish-grey head

olive-green wash to back

plain greyish chest

Length 13 cm **Weight** 20 g
Habitat Forest edges; acacia woodland.
Habits Usually solitary. Unobtrusive; forages in the canopy.

Call (with comparative track)
Similar to that of Lesser Honeyguide, but monosyllabic and lacking the lead-in *teeu*; thus *tik-tik-tik-tik*.

AT A GLANCE

✔ Olive-green wash to back
✔ Plain greyish chest
✔ Plain grey head

Similar-looking species Pallid Honeyguide; Green-backed Honeybird (page 21)

Similar-sounding species Pallid Honeyguide; Zitting Cisticola (page 39)

NOTE Care should be taken when separating this species from Pallid Honeyguide, as the malar stripe is not always visible; head coloration is then a useful feature.

AT A GLANCE

✔ Olive-green wash to back
✔ Plain greyish chest
✔ Plain greenish-grey head

Similar-looking species Lesser Honeyguide; Green-backed Honeybird (page 21)

Similar-sounding species Lesser Honeyguide; Zitting Cisticola (page 39)

NOTE The greenish wash to the head helps to separate this species from Lesser Honeyguide when the malar stripe of the latter is not visible.

Brown-backed Honeybird
Prodotiscus regulus
Skerpbekheuningvoël

Green-backed Honeybird
Prodotiscus zambesiae
Dunbekheuningvoël

brownish-grey back

olive-green wash to back

Length 13 cm **Weight** 14 g
Habitat Open woodland and forest; also savanna.
Habits Usually solitary. Forages in canopy and in grassy areas at edge of forest.

Call (with comparative track)
Cicada-like rattle repeated three or four times.

Length 12 cm **Weight** 12 g
Habitat Teak, miombo and mopane woodland.
Habits Usually solitary. Unobtrusive.

Call
A series of excited chirps, similar to those of a House Sparrow.

STEP TWO – SEPARATING VISUAL GROUPS

True warblers & allied species

Warblers are characterised by having a flattish forehead, unlike the closely related cisticolas and prinias, whose forehead is steeper and head profile is consequently rounded. They constitute a large group of small, drab birds whose coloration varies from rich brown through paler tones to grey and, although some species may have distinctive markings, they are generally difficult to identify on sight alone. Their calls are thus a vital identification tool and it is worthwhile spending time learning them.

Warbling is a descriptive term for rambling birdsong, and it seems apt for the jumbled collection of musical notes that make up warbler calls. The calls may sound quite similar to the beginner, but because of their importance as an aid to identification we regard them as being individually unique (with the exception of those of some reed-warblers) and have included references to similar-sounding species, which you will need to take the time to listen to and familiarise yourself with. This will greatly help you to learn the subtle differences between the calls.

The birds tend to be solitary and are almost always secretive, moving about in reed beds or dense bush without appearing in the open for very long. Although they are often associated with wetlands, many species occur far from this habitat. Most are migratory, spending the summer months in southern Africa. Only a handful of species are found in the region in winter.

Although the Thrush Nightingale is more closely related to the robins, it is included in this group on account of its warbler-like appearance.

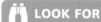

LOOK FOR

✔ call
✔ general upperpart coloration
✔ undertail markings
✔ chest markings
✔ wing coloration/ markings
✔ habitat

Barratt's Warbler

It is worth noting that African and Eurasian reed-warblers are virtually inseparable in the field on plumage and call, and are best distinguished in the hand, where the comparative lengths of the primaries in the folded wing are helpful. The Marsh Warbler is also very similar to these species, but more experienced birders may be able to identify it by the slope of its forehead. The brief glimpse an average birder gets of one of these warblers as it flits around in dense vegetation is unlikely to be helpful in identification, and it is worth remembering that the Marsh Warbler favours a different habitat from that of the two reed-warblers. While the Eurasian Reed-Warbler shares a similar habitat with the African Reed-Warbler, it is a migrant and for the most part present only in summer (although the occurrence of overwintering birds cannot be ruled out). It is also far less common.

WARBLERS CAN BE DIVIDED INTO FOUR VISUAL GROUPS

Broad, heavy tail, no white outer-tail feathers (page 24)

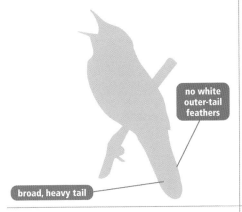

no white outer-tail feathers

broad, heavy tail

Thin tail, no white outer-tail feathers, large size (page 27)

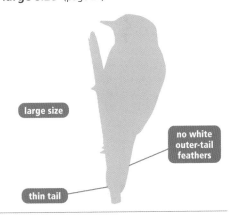

large size

no white outer-tail feathers

thin tail

Thin tail, no white outer-tail feathers, small size (page 30)

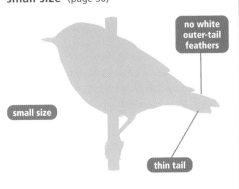

no white outer-tail feathers

small size

thin tail

Thin tail, white on outer-tail feathers (page 34)

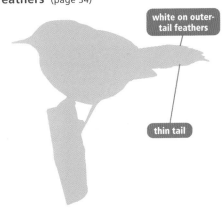

white on outer-tail feathers

thin tail

Typical habitats for this visual group

Little Rush-Warbler is strictly a reed-bed species.

River Warbler is found in denser habitats near water.

Barratt's Warbler is restricted to denser escarpment forest and scrub.

Little Rush-Warbler
Bradypterus baboecala
Kaapse Vleisanger

pale belly with dirty wash

scruffy tail with chestnut undertail coverts

Length 17 cm **Weight** 14 g
Habitat Reed beds and flooded tall grassland.
Habits Secretive and difficult to see, but sometimes perches openly, especially in early mornings.

Call
A series of chirps with a distinctive tone, accelerating and sounding like a playing card against the spokes of a bicycle wheel as it speeds up.

AT A GLANCE

✔ Scruffy tail with chestnut undertail coverts
✔ Pale belly with dirty wash
✔ Habitat
✔ Call

 Similar-looking species Barratt's and Knysna warblers (page 25)

 Similar-sounding species None

NOTE Aside from its distinctive call, this is the only warbler in the group to have an overall grubby appearance and a heavy, often scruffy-looking tail, and to be found in reed beds. Although Knysna and Barratt's warblers also have heavy tails, they are not found in reed beds.

Barratt's Warbler
Bradypterus barratti
Ruigtesanger

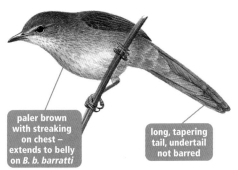

paler brown with streaking on chest – extends to belly on *B. b. barratti*

long, tapering tail, undertail not barred

Length 15 cm **Weight** 15 g

Habitat Dense scrub and other low vegetation along streams and forest edges. May also be found in ouhout thickets along the eastern escarpment.

Habits Remains low in vegetation, often making it necessary to get down on hands and knees to see it.

Call (with comparative track)
Two or three introductory *cheep* notes followed by a metallic warble. Gets to the warble much more quickly than Knysna Warbler does.

║▌║▌║▌║▌║▌║▌║▌║║▌▌ ║▌║ ▌▌▌

AT A GLANCE

✔ Long, tapering tail, undertail not barred
✔ Paler brown with streaking on chest – extends to belly on *B. b. barratti*
✔ Habitat

Similar-looking species Knysna Warbler; Little Rush-Warbler (page 24)

Similar-sounding species Knysna Warbler

NOTE Fairly distinctive in appearance and behaviour, but the call is still the best guide. There is a slight range overlap with Knysna Warbler along the Eastern Cape coast, but the two species can be separated on the shape of the tail.

Knysna Warbler
Bradypterus sylvaticus
Knysnaruigtesanger

square-ended tail, undertail not barred

dark chocolate-brown, with indistinct mottling on chest

Length 15 cm **Weight** 21 g

Habitat Dense, tangled scrub along rivers and forest edges. Absent from forest in which large trees prevent dense undergrowth.

Habits Very secretive and emerges only in response to other species' alarm calls.

Call (with comparative track)
A series of increasingly fast *cheep* notes followed by a short metallic rattle. Takes much longer to get going than Barratt's Warbler does.

║▌║▌║▌║▌║▌║▌║║▌║▌║▌║▌ ▌▌

AT A GLANCE

✔ Square-ended tail, undertail not barred
✔ Dark chocolate-brown, with indistinct mottling on chest
✔ Habitat

Similar-looking species Barratt's Warbler; Little Rush-Warbler (page 24)

Similar-sounding species Barratt's Warbler

NOTE Although the dark brown coloration is an important feature, the call is still the best guide. There is a slight range overlap with Barratt's Warbler along the Eastern Cape coast, but the two species can be separated on the shape of the tail.

River Warbler
Locustella fluviatilis
Sprinkaansanger

broad, rounded tail, barred only on undertail coverts

Length 13 cm
Weight 16 g
Habitat Very dense vegetation along streams. When migrating, also found in isolated thickets.
Habits Very shy and difficult to find. Drops to the ground when disturbed.

Call (with comparative track)
A metallic rattle, similar to that of an insect, or a tambourine being shaken.

▌▌▐▌▌▐▌▌▌▐▌▌▌▐▌▌▌▌▌▐▌▌▌

AT A GLANCE

✔ Broad, rounded tail, barred only on undertail coverts
✔ Call

 Similar-looking species None (streaked throat and chest and partially barred undertail are distinctive)

 Similar-sounding species Brown-backed Honeybird (page 21); White-winged Widowbird (page 121)

NOTE A rare summer migrant (January to April).

Broad-tailed Warbler
Schoenicola brevirostris
Breëstertsanger

broad, rounded tail, barred along entire undertail

Length 15 cm
Weight 15 g
Habitat Tall grass in damp areas and along drainage lines.
Habits Keeps low in vegetation, but may perch in the open early in the morning.

Call

▌▌▐▌▌▐▌▌▐▌▐▌▌▐▌▌▌ ▐▌ ▐▌

A high-pitched metallic *tseep*, almost like a frog or a ship's sonar.

AT A GLANCE

✔ Broad, rounded tail, barred along entire undertail
✔ Call

 Similar-looking species None (white throat and fully barred undertail are distinctive)

 Similar-sounding species None

Typical habitats for this visual group

Great Reed-Warbler is found in a wide range of habitats, from pans to gardens.

Thrush Nightingale occurs in denser woodland habitats.

Lesser Swamp-Warbler is almost exclusively a reed-bed bird.

Thrush Nightingale
Luscinia luscinia
Lysternagtegaal

indistinct to no supercilium

indistinct streaking or mottling on dirty greyish underparts

Length 16 cm **Weight** 25 g

Habitat Dense thickets near rivers, particularly in acacia woodland and on drier ground.

Habits Forages in dense vegetation. Although not necessarily shy, prefers to remain hidden.

Call

Very warbler-like, but with a distinctive deep churring element that gives it a robin-like quality. The combination of robin-like notes with clicks and rattles is unique.

AT A GLANCE

✔ Indistinct to no supercilium
✔ Indistinct streaking or mottling on dirty greyish underparts
✔ Habitat
✔ Call

 Similar-looking species None (rich coloration of rump and tail is distinctive)

 Similar-sounding species None

NOTE A summer migrant (December to March).

Basra Reed-Warbler
Acrocephalus griseldis
Basrarietsanger

Great Reed-Warbler
Acrocephalus arundinaceus
Grootrietsanger

bold supercilium

long, thin bill, strikingly pointed

bulky size

bold supercilium

long, thick bill

bulky size (heaviest in the group)

Length 16 cm
Weight 18 g
Habitat Reed beds and bushwillow thickets near water.
Habits Less secretive than other reed-warblers. The only reed-warbler that forages in tree canopies.

Call (with comparative track)
Given in short bursts. Similar to that of the Great Reed-Warbler but less scratchy and less well defined. Reminiscent of starling calls.

Length 19 cm **Weight** 32 g
Habitat A wide range, from reed beds to acacia woodland; includes maize and other croplands. Often far from water.
Habits Forages low in vegetation, rarely perching in the open.

Call (with comparative track)
A series of scratchy warbler notes; no other warbler call sounds as harsh. Loud and far-carrying.

AT A GLANCE

✔ Bold supercilium
✔ Bulky size
✔ Long, thin bill, strikingly pointed
✔ Call

 Similar-looking species Greater Swamp-Warbler (page 29); Great Reed-Warbler; Upcher's Warbler (page 34)

 Similar-sounding species Olive-tree Warbler (page 34); Great Reed-Warbler

NOTE Best identified by call. A rare vagrant to the region, recorded mainly in January and February. Only Lesser Swamp-, Greater Swamp- and Basra Reed- may have greyish legs. Any reed-bed warbler with greyish legs will always be a member of this small group.

AT A GLANCE

✔ Bold supercilium
✔ Bulky size (heaviest in the group)
✔ Long, thick bill
✔ Call

 Similar-looking species Greater Swamp-Warbler (page 29); Basra Reed-Warbler

 Similar-sounding species Olive-tree Warbler (page 34); Basra Reed-Warbler; Upcher's Warbler (page 34)

NOTE Although its large size is distinctive, it is still best identified by call. A summer migrant (December to April).

Lesser Swamp-Warbler
Acrocephalus gracilirostris
Kaapse Rietsanger

bold supercilium

small, thin bill, almost Prinia-like

compact size (lighter weight than Basra and Great Reed-)

Length 17 cm **Weight** 15 g
Habitat Reed beds in rivers, dams and estuaries.
Habits Skulks low down among reeds when foraging for insects, which it takes near the water surface. May perch at tops of reeds when not feeding.

Call (with comparative track)
Very full, bubbly and musical, with tuneful notes and yodels. Less harsh and deep than that of Greater Swamp-Warbler.

AT A GLANCE

- ✔ Bold supercilium
- ✔ Compact size (lighter weight than Basra and Great Reed-)
- ✔ Small, thin bill, almost Prinia-like
- ✔ Call

 Similar-looking species None (rust-coloured wash on flanks is distinctive)

 Similar-sounding species Greater Swamp-Warbler

NOTE The leg colour is sometimes dark olive-green but never pinkish or light brown. Only Lesser Swamp-, Greater Swamp- and Basra Reed- may have greyish legs. Any reed-bed warbler with greyish legs will always be a member of this small group.

Greater Swamp-Warbler
Acrocephalus rufescens
Rooibruinrietsanger

indistinct to no supercilium

plain pale cream underparts

Length 18 cm
Weight 20 g
Habitat Papyrus reed beds.
Habits Climbs up and down reed stems as it forages, and hops from one stem to another.

Call (with comparative track)
Full, deep and bubbly. Similar to that of Lesser Swamp-Warbler but more of a chuckle and with more scratchy notes.

AT A GLANCE

- ✔ Indistinct to no supercilium
- ✔ Plain pale cream underparts
- ✔ Habitat
- ✔ Call

 Similar-looking species Basra (page 28) and Great (page 28) reed-warblers

 Similar-sounding species Lesser Swamp-Warbler

NOTE Best identified by call. Confined to a limited range. Only Lesser Swamp-, Greater Swamp- and Basra Reed- may have greyish legs. Any reed-bed warbler with greyish legs will always be a member of this small group.

Willow Warbler
Phylloscopus trochilus
Hofsanger

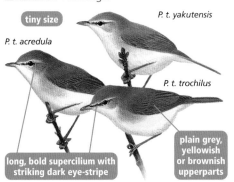

P. t. yakutensis

tiny size

P. t. acredula

P. t. trochilus

plain grey, yellowish or brownish upperparts

long, bold supercilium with striking dark eye-stripe

Length 11 cm **Weight** 9 g
Habitat Most woodland types, from acacia to broad-leaved; also in parks and gardens.
Habits Usually solitary, but sometimes occurs in flocks of up to 20 birds in a tree. Moves around restlessly.

Call   ▌▌▌▌▌▌▌▌▌▌▌▌▌▌▌▌
A rapid floaty and descending series of sweet whistles; also a soft, two-noted *too-it*.

Icterine Warbler
Hippolais icterina
Spotsanger

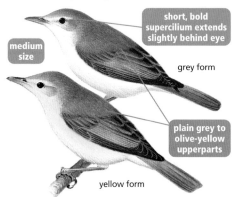

short, bold supercilium extends slightly behind eye

grey form

medium size

plain grey to olive-yellow upperparts

yellow form

Length 14.5 cm **Weight** 12 g
Habitat Woodland and riverine bush.
Habits Usually moves around in the canopy. Shy and easily overlooked.

Call (with comparative track)
Sustained, purposeful medley of typical warbler notes, including 'kissing' sounds, similar to that of a starling.

▌▌▌▌▌▌▌▌▌▌▌▌▌▌▌▌

Garden Warbler
Sylvia borin
Tuinsanger

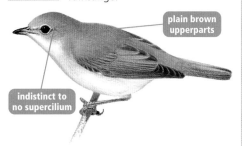

plain brown upperparts

indistinct to no supercilium

Length 14 cm **Weight** 19 g
Habitat Dense vegetation, also in gardens and parks.
Habits Usually solitary, but may occur in small flocks, particularly in trees with soft fruits.

Call (with comparative track)
Very hurried, the notes flowing together with no gaps between them. Similar to Marsh Warbler call but with regular pauses between phrases and no mimicry.

AT A GLANCE
✔ Plain brown upperparts
✔ Indistinct to no supercilium
✔ Call

Similar-looking species None (plain coloration and eye-ring around large eye are distinctive)

Similar-sounding species Marsh Warbler (page 33)

NOTE A summer migrant (October to April).

Sedge Warbler
Acrocephalus schoenobaenus
Europese Vleisanger

boldly streaked upperparts

Length 13 cm **Weight** 12 g
Habitat Mainly in reed beds and tangled undergrowth under wetland trees. Occasionally in gardens.
Habits Shy and reclusive, quickly disappearing into vegetation when disturbed.

Call (with comparative track)
A series of agitated notes. Appears to be trying to copy the repeated phrasing characteristic of reed-warblers but without complete success.

AT A GLANCE
✔ Boldly streaked upperparts
✔ Call

Similar-looking species None

Similar-sounding species African and Eurasian reed-warblers (page 32)

NOTE A summer migrant (October to April).

African Reed-Warbler
Acrocephalus baeticatus
Kleinrietsanger

plain brown upperparts

bold supercilium lacks dark eye-stripe

wing formula (see diagrams)

Length 13 cm **Weight** 11 g
Habitat Usually in reed beds and flooded grassland in summer; drier habitats in winter.
Habits Often overlooked; best located when calling.

Call (with comparative track)
A series of 2–5 repeated notes followed by a different series; often includes mimicry.

▐▌▐▐▐▌▐▐▐▌▐▐▌▐▌ ▐ ▐▌▐

Eurasian Reed-Warbler
Acrocephalus scirpaceus
Hermanse Rietsanger

bold supercilium lacks dark eye-stripe

plain brown upperparts

wing formula (see diagrams)

Length 13 cm
Weight 11 g
Habitat Usually in reed beds and flooded grassland.
Habits Skulks in vegetation and is easily overlooked. Best located when calling.

Call (with comparative track)
A series of 2–5 repeated notes followed by a different series; often includes mimicry.

▐▌▐▐▐▐▐▌▐▐▌▐▐ ▐▌ ▐▐▌ ▐▌▐

Marsh Warbler
Acrocephalus palustris
Europese Rietsanger

plain brown upperparts

bold supercilium lacks dark eye-stripe

wing formula (see diagrams)

Length 13 cm **Weight** 12 g
Habitat Dense, tangled vegetation in woodland, parks and gardens.
Habits Skulks, often calling from deep within tangled vegetation.

Call (with comparative track)
Very hurried but with slower sections, as if resting; includes many mimicked sounds, but with no pattern or structure (the similar-sounding Garden Warbler does not mimic).

AT A GLANCE

✔ Plain brown upperparts
✔ Bold supercilium lacks dark eye-stripe
✔ Wing formula (see diagrams)
✔ Call

Similar-looking species African and Eurasian reed-warblers (page 32)

Similar-sounding species Garden Warbler (page 31)

NOTE A typical warbler and very similar to African and Eurasian reed-warblers; best identified by call. When not calling, detailed measurements and wing formula from a bird in the hand are the best guide. A summer migrant (November to April).

Wing formulas

African Reed-Warbler

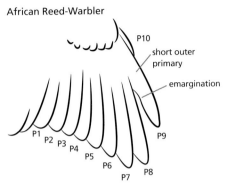

P10
short outer primary
emargination
P1 P2 P3 P4 P5 P6 P7 P8 P9

Eurasian Reed-Warbler

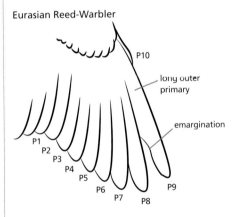

P10
long outer primary
emargination
P1 P2 P3 P4 P5 P6 P7 P8 P9

Marsh Warbler

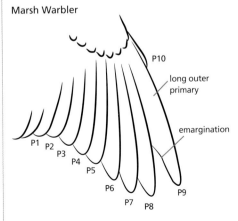

P10
long outer primary
emargination
P1 P2 P3 P4 P5 P6 P7 P8 P9

Source: *Sasol Birds of Southern Africa*

Olive-tree Warbler
Hippolais olivetorum
Olyfboomsanger

longer wing (primary projection >80% length of tertials)

contrasting pale wing panel

outer three tail feathers tipped white (resembles scrub robin tail)

Length 17 cm **Weight** 18 g
Habitat Acacia woodland with tall trees.
Habits Solitary and shy, but responds to spishing.

Call (with comparative track)
Very full and bold, with a deep, liquid character;
includes some grating sounds. Similar to the calls
of swamp-warblers, but less musical.

AT A GLANCE

✔ Contrasting pale wing panel
✔ Longer wing (primary projection >80%
length of tertials)
✔ Outer three tail feathers tipped white
(resembles scrub robin tail)
✔ Call

 Similar-looking species Upcher's
Warbler

 Similar-sounding species Basra and
Great reed-warblers (page 28); Upcher's
Warbler

NOTE A summer migrant (November to April).

Upcher's Warbler
Hippolais languida
Vaalspotsanger

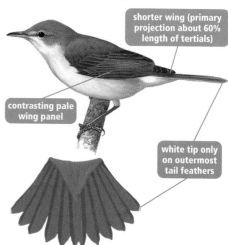

shorter wing (primary projection about 60% length of tertials)

contrasting pale wing panel

white tip only on outermost tail feathers

Length 15 cm **Weight** 12 g
Habitat Semi-arid savanna and thickets.
Habits Solitary and regularly perches and
feeds openly.

Call (with comparative track)
The only southern African record to date called
with chat-like *chuk* notes. Song, which may be
heard in the region, is a liquid, bubbly call similar
to that of Olive-tree but more wheatear-like.

AT A GLANCE

✔ Contrasting pale wing panel
✔ Shorter wing (primary projection about
60% length of tertials)
✔ White tip only on outermost tail feathers
✔ Call

 Similar-looking species Olive-tree
Warbler

 Similar-sounding species Basra and
Great reed-warblers (page 28); Olive-
tree Warbler, but song resembles the
call of a wheatear or chat.

NOTE A summer migrant (November to April).

Common Whitethroat
Sylvia communis
Witkeelsanger

rufous wing panel

Length 14 cm **Weight** 15 g
Habitat Dry acacia or broad-leaved woodland.
Habits Skulks in low vegetation, raising crest when agitated. Flies low and fast between patches of dense bush.

Call (with comparative track)
A rapid jumble of sunbird-like sounds with no low-pitched notes. Song often comprises short phrases with gaps between them, like that of the Greater Double-collared Sunbird.

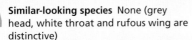

AT A GLANCE

✔ Rufous wing panel
✔ Call

Similar-looking species None (grey head, white throat and rufous wing are distinctive)

Similar-sounding species None

NOTE A summer migrant (November to April).

Typical habitats for this visual group

The Sedge Warbler is a common summer visitor to most reed beds.

Warblers that occupy dense thickets, such as the Thrush Nightingale, can be rather difficult to locate.

Acacia woodland, where the Common Whitethroat occurs, is not usually associated with warblers.

Cisticolas

Cisticolas are small birds that could be described as a cross between prinias and warblers. Unlike the latter, which have a flat forehead, cisticolas have a rounded head and this, in addition to a plumper body, helps to distinguish them. The Red-winged Warbler, however, could be confused with some of the plain-backed cisticolas and is therefore included in this group.

In general the plumage tends to be overall brown with paler underparts, and it is only tail length and differing colours and patterns on the back that help to identify species. Whereas in some species the back is plain, in others it is distinctively marked; in the latter it is important to appreciate the subtle difference between a black back with grey streaks (where black is the predominant colour, as in Levaillant's Cisticola) and a grey back with black streaks (where grey is the predominant colour, as in Wailing Cisticola). It is also useful to note that some species have a slightly different breeding plumage, so it helps to be aware of the time of year that they breed. Many cisticolas have longer tails and appear browner in winter.

Because many of the species look similar, call is important when identifying them – in some instances it is the only way to separate them in the field. Habitat is another clue, as many species are sedentary and usually habitat-bound. All species prefer a significant grassy component in the habitat, even when they occur along forest edges. Be aware that when on the move, these species may sometimes be found outside of their usual habitat. Although often found in the open, cisticolas very seldom occur on the ground. They frequently perch conspicuously and dart around energetically. In the breeding season most of the short-tailed species perform aerial displays, during which they call. The combination of display and call is often the best way to separate these species.

LOOK FOR

✔ tail length and pattern
✔ main colour of back
✔ habitat
✔ call
✔ habits

Pale-crowned Cisticola

Short tail, boldly marked back (page 39)

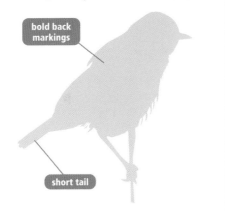

bold back markings

short tail

Plain back (page 43)

plain back

Long tail, bold markings on brown back (page 47)

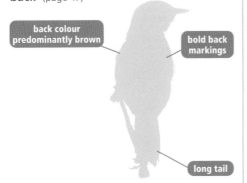

back colour predominantly brown

bold back markings

long tail

Long tail, bold markings on black back (page 52)

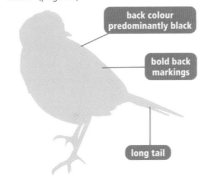

back colour predominantly black

bold back markings

long tail

Grey back with markings (page 54)

grey back marked with noticeable to bold markings

Neddicky can be surprisingly tricky to identify.

Flight patterns of the cloud scraper cisticolas

A better understanding of both the calls and the flight paths of the cloud scraper cisticolas is very helpful for making a positive identification. Below we outline the flight paths, with call descriptions overlaid to aid identification. Pay careful attention to the height above the ground: some, like Zitting and Desert, display quite low and can be seen, while others, like Cloud and Pale-crowned, display very high and are hard to see while overhead.

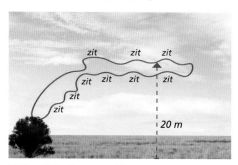

Zitting Cisticola – up to 20 m

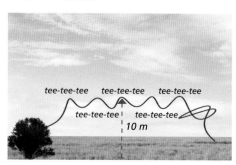

Desert Cisticola – up to 10 m

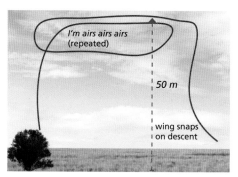

Wing-snapping Cisticola – > 50 m

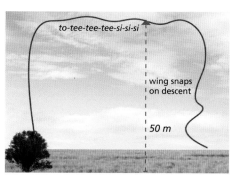

Cloud Cisticola – > 50 m

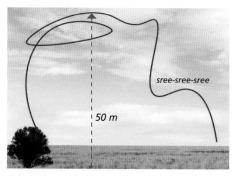

Pale-crowned Cisticola – > 50 m

Zitting Cisticola calls during an aerial display.

Zitting Cisticola
Cisticola juncidis
Landeryklopkloppie

streaked crown

thin bill

Length 11 cm **Weight** 9 g
Habitat Grasslands, especially where grass is up to waist height. Often around golf courses and fallow farmland, which it favours when found in arid areas.
Habits Usually secretive, but perches on grass stems when disturbed. Performs bobbing aerial display in breeding season. See display flight pattern on page 38.

Call (with comparative track)
A piercing, metallic *zit-zit-zit* repeated during aerial display. Also a fast, agitated 'ticking' alarm call, similar to that of other members of this group.

✔ Streaked crown
✔ Thin bill
✔ Call

 Similar-looking species Desert, Cloud (page 40), Wing-snapping (page 41), Pale-crowned (page 41) and Short-winged non-breeding (page 42) cisticolas

 Similar-sounding species Lesser and Pallid honeyguides (page 20)

NOTE A common and widespread species that is difficult to identify in the field. The call is the best guide.

Desert Cisticola
Cisticola aridulus
Woestynklopkloppie

streaked crown

thin bill

Length 11 cm **Weight** 9 g
Habitat Dry grassland with scattered trees and bushes. Also crop land. Habitat usually has patches of dry ground.
Habits Solitary or in small groups. Calls from an open perch and during its bouncing aerial display, when it often includes single wing clicks. See display flight pattern on page 38.

Call (with comparative track)
A series of piercing notes at the same pitch, *tee-tee-tee....* The pitch may vary from one call to the next, but it remains constant within one phrase. Also staccato notes mixed with wing clicks, like a Neddicky.

✔ Streaked crown
✔ Thin bill
✔ Call

 Similar-looking species Zitting, Cloud (page 40), Wing-snapping (page 41), Pale-crowned non-breeding (page 41) and Short-winged non-breeding (page 42) cisticolas

 Similar-sounding species Cloud and Wing-snapping cisticolas (page 40); Neddicky (page 43)

NOTE Very difficult to identify in the field; call is the best guide.

Cloud Cisticola
Cisticola textrix
Gevlekte Klopkloppie

C.t. textrix

C.t. major & marleyi

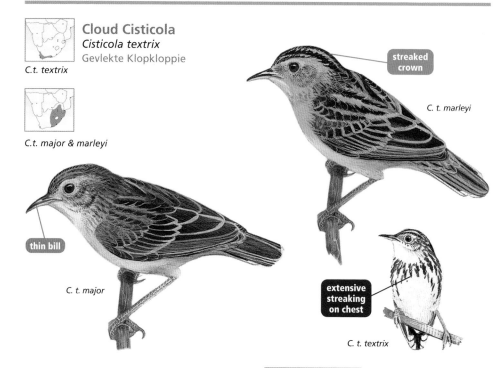

C. t. marleyi

streaked crown

thin bill

C. t. major

extensive streaking on chest

C. t. textrix

Length 11 cm **Weight** 9 g

Habitat Short grassland with bare patches.

Habits Secretive, except in the breeding season. Its display flight is level, ending in a dive that is accompanied by rapid clicking. See display flight pattern on page 38.

Call (with comparative track)

Similar to that of Wing-snapping Cisticola, sometimes with an additional higher note at the end followed by a rapid *chik-chik-chik-chik-chik* that may sound like a wing snap. Also *to-tee-tee-tee-si-si* repeated several times and ending in a rapid *chik-chik-chik-chik-chik*.

AT A GLANCE

All races except *C. t. textrix*
✔ Streaked crown
✔ Thin bill
✔ Call

C. t. textrix (southwestern Cape form)
✔ Extensive chest streaking
✔ Call

 Similar-looking species Zitting (page 39), Desert (page 39), Wing-snapping (page 41), Pale-crowned non-breeding (page 41) and Short-winged non-breeding (page 42) cisticolas

 Similar-sounding species Desert (page 39) and Wing-snapping (page 41) cisticolas; Neddicky (page 43)

NOTE Very difficult to identify in the field; call is best guide. Birds in southern and southwestern Cape show streaking across chest. Male has longer legs than other species in group, but as there is little differentiation in leg length among females, this is of interest rather than an identifying feature.

Wing-snapping Cisticola
Cisticola ayresii
Kleinste Klopkloppie

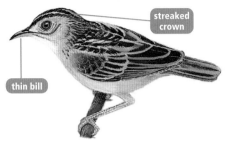

streaked crown

thin bill

Length 10 cm **Weight** 10 g
Habitat Short grassland, especially where there are bare patches and grass is frequently grazed.
Habits Solitary or in pairs. Secretive, except when performing its undulating display flights in the breeding season. See display flight pattern on page 38.

Call (with comparative track)
Ringing, high-pitched *I'm-airs-airs-airs* interspersed with wing snaps. The *I'm* is not always audible.

AT A GLANCE

✔ Streaked crown
✔ Thin bill
✔ Call

Similar-looking species Zitting (page 39), Desert (page 39), Cloud (page 40) and Pale-crowned cisticolas

Similar-sounding species Desert (page 39) and Cloud (page 40) cisticolas; Neddicky (page 43)

NOTE Very difficult to identify in the field; the call is the best guide.

Pale-crowned Cisticola
Cisticola cinnamomeus
Bleekkopklopkloppie

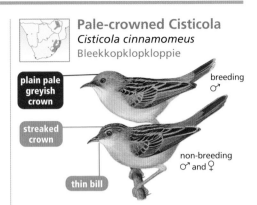

breeding ♂

plain pale greyish crown

streaked crown

non-breeding ♂ and ♀

thin bill

Length 11 cm **Weight** 10 g
Habitat Short, moist grassland and grassy pans.
Habits Secretive, except in the breeding season. Perches on grass stem when disturbed. The display flight is undulating, with a repetitive call given at the top of each curve and three cricket-like trills in the dip.

Call
A metallic chatter. Also an almost laughing *tsee-tsee-tsee-tsee* and a trilling, cricket-like *srrrree-ssrrrreee-srreeee*.

AT A GLANCE

Female and non-breeding male
✔ Streaked crown
✔ Thin bill
✔ Call
Breeding male
✔ Plain pale greyish crown
✔ Call

Similar-looking species to non-breeding plumage Zitting (page 39), Desert (page 39), Cloud (page 40), Wing-snapping and Short-winged non-breeding (page 42) cisticolas

Similar-sounding species None

NOTE The pale crown is diagnostic in breeding males. With their blackish-streaked crowns, females and non-breeding males are very similar to the other cisticolas indicated; the call is the best guide.

Croaking Cisticola
(breeding female)
Cisticola natalensis
Groottinktinkie

streaked crown

large size

strong, heavy bill

Short-winged Cisticola
(non-breeding)
Cisticola brachypterus
Kortvlerktinktinkie

streaked crown

thin bill

Length 15 cm
Weight 18 g
Habitat Moist grassland with scattered bushes, especially around pans. Also forest clearings.
Habits Secretive, but perches in the open and gives an alarm call when disturbed. Neighbouring males call from conspicuous perches during the breeding season.

Call
Females and males give similar harsh alarm calls.

Length 11 cm **Weight** 9 g
Habitat Clearings in and edges of miombo woodland, especially with dead trees.
Habits Usually secretive, but perches in the open when disturbed.

Call
A mixture of sunbird-like and other melodic notes, uncharacteristic for a cisticola.

Lazy Cisticola
(all races except *C. a. aberrans*)
Cisticola aberrans
Luitinktinkie

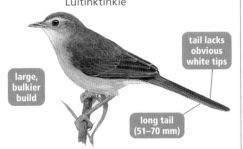

large, bulkier build

tail lacks obvious white tips

long tail (51–70 mm)

Length 14 cm **Weight** 14 g
Habitat Rocky areas with grass and scattered bushes; forest edges.
Habits Clambers about secretively, mouse-like. Cocks tail when calling.

Call
A shrill squeal, like a rubber toy being squeezed, mixed with buzzing and clicking notes.

AT A GLANCE
✔ Tail lacks obvious white tips
✔ Long tail (51–70 mm)
✔ Large, bulkier build
✔ Call

Similar-looking species None (the long tail and rich rufous crown are distinctive)

Similar-sounding species None

Neddicky
Cisticola fulvicapilla
Neddikkie

short tail (35–44 mm)

tiny build

tail lacks obvious white tips

Length 10 cm **Weight** 9 g
Habitat Broad-leaved woodland, rocky areas with scrubby growth, and plantations.
Habits Usually solitary or in small flocks. More conspicuous when vocal.

Call (with comparative track)
Repeated staccato *stuk-stuk-stuk* notes; piercing whistles similar to the call of Red-crested Korhaan, but without clicks; and a series of *si-si-si-si* notes reminiscent of Desert Cisticola.

AT A GLANCE
✔ Tail lacks obvious white tips
✔ Short tail (35–44 mm)
✔ Tiny build
✔ Call

Similar-looking species None (the shorter tail and rich rufous crown are distinctive)

Similar-sounding species Desert (page 39), Cloud (page 40) and Wing-snapping (page 41) cisticolas

NOTE Although call may resemble that of other cisticolas, Neddicky does not perform aerial displays.

Rattling Cisticola
(breeding)
Cisticola chiniana procerus
Bosveldtinktinkie

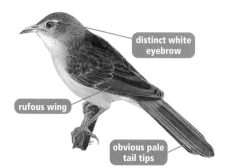

distinct white eyebrow

rufous wing

obvious pale tail tips

Length 15 cm **Weight** 15 g
Habitat Acacia woodland, patches of bush in grassland and sometimes gardens.
Habits Conspicuous for a cisticola and easy to find all year. Calls from the top of bushes and trees.

Call

Harsh rattling sounds introduced by notes such as *zee-zee-zee*, showing much variation.

AT A GLANCE

✔ Obvious pale tail tips
✔ Distinct white eyebrow
✔ Rufous wing
✔ **Call**

 Similar-looking species None (the brown tail is a useful additional feature)

Similar-sounding species None

Singing Cisticola
Cisticola cantans
Singende Tinktinkie

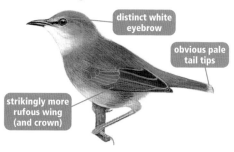

distinct white eyebrow

obvious pale tail tips

strikingly more rufous wing (and crown)

Length 13 cm **Weight** 13 g
Habitat Along streams, in bracken and other moist vegetation among trees and bushes.
Habits Secretive; easiest to find during the breeding season.

Call (with comparative track)
A series of widely spaced, sparrow-like chirps.

AT A GLANCE

✔ Obvious pale tail tips
✔ Distinct white eyebrow
✔ Strikingly more rufous wing and crown

 Similar-looking species (to non-breeding plumage) Red-faced Cisticola (page 45)

 Similar-sounding species Rufous-winged and Luapula cisticolas (page 52)

Red-faced Cisticola
Cisticola erythrops
Rooiwangtinktinkie

no obvious eyebrow

plain wing lacks striking rufous panel

obvious pale tail tips

Length 14 cm **Weight** 15 g
Habitat Reed beds and other tall vegetation along streams. Sometimes strays into riverine woodland.
Habits Somewhat secretive, but very vocal in breeding season.

Call
A series of loud, excited whistles, each lower in pitch than the previous one. Also a series of excited trills.

AT A GLANCE
✔ Obvious pale tail tips
✔ No obvious eyebrow
✔ Plain wing lacks striking rufous panel
✔ Call

Similar-looking species Singing Cisticola (page 44)

Similar-sounding species None

Short-winged Cisticola
(breeding)
Cisticola brachypterus
Kortvlerktinktinkie

no obvious eyebrow

mottled wing lacks rufous wing panel

obvious pale tail tips

Length 11 cm **Weight** 9 g
Habitat Clearings in and edges of miombo woodland, especially with dead trees.
Habits Usually secretive, but perches in the open when disturbed.

Call
A mixture of sunbird-like and other melodic notes, uncharacteristic for a cisticola.

AT A GLANCE
✔ Obvious pale tail tips
✔ No obvious eyebrow
✔ Mottled wing lacks rufous wing panel
✔ Call

Similar-looking species None (short bill and overall olive appearance are distinctive)

Similar-sounding species None

Red-winged Warbler
(non-breeding male)
Heliolais erythropterus
Rooivlerksanger

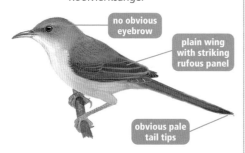

no obvious eyebrow

plain wing with striking rufous panel

obvious pale tail tips

Typical habitats for this visual group

The best place to look for Neddicky is in open woodland in hilly areas.

Length 14 cm **Weight** 12 g
Habitat Miombo woodland with long grass, forest edges and dense riverine bush.
Habits Usually in pairs or small flocks. Moves constantly through vegetation close to the ground, calling to keep in contact with the rest of the group.

Call ▮▮▮▮▮▮▮▮ ▮▮▮▮▮▮ ▮▮▮▮ ▮ ▮▮▮
A series of excited chirps, similar to those of a petronia, repeated at the same pitch.

Rattling Cisticola is very common in acacia woodland.

Boulder-strewn slopes are the favoured habitat of Lazy Cisticola.

AT A GLANCE

✔ Obvious pale tail tips
✔ No obvious eyebrow
✔ Plain wing with striking rufous panel
✔ Call

 Similar-looking species None (the bold rufous wing panel is distinctive)

 Similar-sounding species None

Chirping Cisticola
Cisticola pipiens
Piepende Tinktinkie

best identified on habitat, distribution and call

Length 14 cm **Weight** 16 g
Habitat Flooded grassland pans and reed beds.
Habits Usually shy and quiet out of breeding season, but may sun itself in the open in the early mornings.

Call (with comparative track)
Two or three *tik* notes followed by a cicada-like buzz. Also some plaintive whistles.

AT A GLANCE

✔ Habitat
✔ Distribution
✔ Call

 Similar-looking species All in this group except Croaking Cisticola (page 50), which has a much heavier bill.

 Similar-sounding species Grey-backed (page 49), Tinkling (page 49) and Wailing (page 51) cisticolas

NOTE The whistles are similar to those of Gabar Goshawk.

 Rufous-winged Cisticola
(non-breeding)
Cisticola galactotes
Swartrugtinktinkie

best identified on habitat, distribution and call

Length 13 cm **Weight** 13 g
Habitat Reed beds around pans and dams.
Habits Secretive when not breeding, keeping low in vegetation.

Call (with comparative track)
A series of closely spaced, petronia-like chirps.

AT A GLANCE

✔ Habitat
✔ Distribution
✔ Call

 Similar-looking species All in this group except Croaking Cisticola (page 50), which has a much heavier bill.

 Similar-sounding species Singing Cisticola (page 44)

Luapula Cisticola
(non-breeding)
Cisticola luapula
Luapulatinktinkie

best identified on habitat, distribution and call

Length 13 cm **Weight** 13 g
Habitat Reed beds and other flooded aquatic vegetation.
Habits Secretive when not breeding.

Call (with comparative track)
A series of closely spaced chirps similar to a House Sparrow.

AT A GLANCE

✔ Habitat
✔ Distribution
✔ Call

Similar-looking species All in this group except Croaking Cisticola (page 50), which has a much heavier bill.

Similar-sounding species House Sparrow (page 126)

Levaillant's Cisticola
(non-breeding)
Cisticola tinniens
Vleitinktinkie

best identified on habitat, distribution and call

Length 14 cm **Weight** 12 g
Habitat Reed beds and tall grass in marshy areas. Sometimes also in tall grassland in montane areas, such as Suikerbosrand. Not only a 'wetland Cisticola'.
Habits Very visible and vocal in the breeding season. Quieter and more secretive when not breeding.

Call
A distinctive and bubbly *chip-turalura-lip*. Also a shrill and excited alarm call.

AT A GLANCE

✔ Habitat
✔ Distribution
✔ Call

 Similar-looking species All in this group except Croaking Cisticola (page 50), which has a much heavier bill.

 Similar-sounding species None

NOTE Non-breeding birds are best separated on call.

Grey-backed Cisticola
(*C. s. windhoekensis* and
C.s. newtoni)
Cisticola subruficapilla
Grysrugtinktinkie

best identified on
habitat, distribution
and call

Tinkling Cisticola
Cisticola rufilatus
Rooitinktinkie

best identified on
habitat, distribution
and call

Length 14 cm **Weight** 14 g
Habitat Dry savanna with scattered trees, and
edges of miombo woodland on deep sandy soils.
Habits Very shy, dropping down into vegetation
and running like a mouse when disturbed.

Call (with comparative track)
A thin, metallic rattle with some introductory
chuck notes. Also a series of piercing whistles.

Length 13 cm
Weight 10 g
Habitat Shrubland and
grassy patches on rocky
slopes in arid areas.
Habits Frequently
perches in the open.

Call (with comparative track)
A slow, bubbly rattle, occasionally with a few
introductory *chuck* notes. Also a series of
piercing whistles.

AT A GLANCE

 ✔ Habitat
✔ Distribution
✔ Call

 Similar-looking species All in this group
except Croaking Cisticola (page 50),
which has a heavier bill.

Similar-sounding species Chirping
(page 47), Tinkling and Wailing
(page 51) cisticolas

NOTE Although Wailing Cisticola is similar, it
has 'warmer' (browner) underparts.

AT A GLANCE

 ✔ Habitat
✔ Distribution
✔ Call

 Similar-looking species All in this group
except Croaking Cisticola (page 50),
which has a much heavier bill.

Similar-sounding species Chirping
(page 47), Grey-backed and Wailing
(page 51) cisticolas

Croaking Cisticola
(non-breeding male)
Cisticola natalensis
Groottinktinkie

best identified on habitat, distribution and call

Length 15 cm **Weight** 25 g
Habitat Moist grassland with scattered bushes, especially around pans. Also forest clearings.
Habits Secretive, but perches in the open and gives an alarm call when disturbed.

Call
A range of loud, frog-like croaks and buzzes.

NOTE See also breeding female (page 42) and breeding male (page 54).

AT A GLANCE

✔ Habitat
✔ Distribution
✔ Call

Similar-looking species None (heavy bill is distinctive)

Similar-sounding species None

Rattling Cisticola
(All except *C. c. frater* and *C. c. procerus* breeding)
Cisticola chiniana
Bosveldtinktinkie

best identified on habitat, distribution and call

Length 15 cm **Weight** 15 g
Habitat Acacia woodland, patches of bush in grassland and sometimes gardens.
Habits Conspicuous for a cisticola and easy to find all year. Calls from the top of bushes and trees.

Call
Harsh rattling sounds introduced by notes such as *zee-zee-zee*, showing much variation.

AT A GLANCE

✔ Habitat
✔ Distribution
✔ Call

Similar-looking species All in this group except Croaking Cisticola, which has a much heavier bill.

Similar-sounding species None

Wailing Cisticola
(*C. l. mashona* and *C. l. monticola*)
Cisticola lais
Huiltinktinkie

best identified on habitat, distribution and call

Length 12 cm **Weight** 15 g
Habitat Montane grassy slopes with scattered bushes and bracken.
Habits Perches in the open, frequently at the top of a prominent bush.

Call (with comparative track)
A buzzy rattle, with one or two introductory *chuck* notes. Also a series of piercing whistles.

AT A GLANCE
✔ Habitat
✔ Distribution
✔ Call

 Similar-looking species All in this group except Croaking Cisticola (page 50), which has a much heavier bill.

 Similar-sounding species Grey-backed and Tinkling cisticolas (page 49)

NOTE Although the Grey-backed Cisticola is similar, it has 'colder' (greyer) underparts.

Habitat & distribution quick reference

 Chirping Cisticola
Habitat Flooded grassland pans and reed beds

 Rufous-winged Cisticola non-br.
Habitat Reed beds around pans and dams

 Luapula Cisticola non-br.
Habitat Reed beds and other flooded aquatic vegetation

 Levaillant's Cisticola non-br.
Habitat Reed beds and tall grass in marshy areas, sometimes in tall grassland in montane areas

 Grey-backed Cisticola
(*C. s. windhoekensis* and *C. s. newtoni*)
Habitat Shrubland and grassy patches on rocky slopes in arid areas

 Tinkling Cisticola
Habitat Dry savanna with scattered trees, and edges of miombo woodland on deep sandy soils

 Croaking Cisticola non-br. male
Habitat Moist grassland with scattered bushes, especially around pans; also forest clearings

 Rattling Cisticola
(All races except *C. c. frater* and *C.c. procerus* breeding)
Habitat Acacia woodland, patches of bush in grassland and sometimes gardens

 Wailing Cisticola
(*C. l. mashona* and *C. l. monticola*)
Habitat Montane grassy slopes with scattered bushes and bracken

Rufous-winged Cisticola
(breeding)
Cisticola galactotes
Swartrugtinktinkie

grey tail

Length 12 cm **Weight** 13 g
Habitat Reed beds around pans and dams.
Habits Secretive when not breeding, keeping low in vegetation.

Call (with comparative track)
A series of closely spaced, petronia-like chirps.

AT A GLANCE

✔ Grey tail
✔ Distribution
✔ Call

 Similar-looking species Luapula and Levaillant's (page 53) cisticolas in breeding plumage

 Similar-sounding species Singing Cisticola (page 44)

NOTE Grey tail only relevant in breeding plumage. Non-breeding has a browner tail but back markings differ and place it in another visual group.

Luapula Cisticola
(breeding)
Cisticola luapula
Luapulatinktinkie

grey tail

Length 12 cm **Weight** 13 g
Habitat Reed beds and other flooded aquatic vegetation.
Habits Secretive when not breeding.

Call (with comparative track)
Chip chip chip chip, similar to the single notes of the House Sparrow.

AT A GLANCE

✔ Grey tail
✔ Distribution
✔ Call

 Similar-looking species Rufous-winged and Levaillant's (page 53) cisticolas in breeding plumage

 Similar-sounding species House Sparrow (page 126)

NOTE Grey tail only relevant in breeding plumage. Non-breeding has a browner tail but back markings differ and place it in another visual group.

Levaillant's Cisticola
(breeding)
Cisticola tinniens
Vleitinktinkie

rufous tail

Length 13 cm **Weight** 12 g
Habitat Reed beds and tall grass in marshy areas. Sometimes also in tall grassland in montane areas, such as Suikerbosrand. Not only a 'wetland Cisticola'.
Habits Visible and vocal in the breeding season. Quieter and more secretive when not breeding.

Call ▐█▐█▐█▐▐ █▐██▐█ ▐█ ▐▐█
A distinctive and bubbly *chip-turalura-lip*. Also a shrill and excited alarm call.

Typical habitats for this visual group

ABOVE AND TOP: *Some cisticolas, such as Levaillant's Cisticola, can occur in a wide range of habitats, from reed beds to rank montane grassland. The other members of this group, namely Rufous-winged and Luapula cisticolas, tend to be more habitat bound and are found only in suitable reed-bed habitats.*

AT A GLANCE

✔ Rufous tail
✔ Call

 Similar-looking species Rufous-winged and Luapula cisticolas (page 52) in breeding plumage

 Similar-sounding species None

NOTE Rufous tail only relevant in breeding plumage. Non-breeding Luapula and Rufous-winged cisticolas have browner tails but back markings differ and place them in another visual group.

Croaking Cisticola
(breeding male)
Cisticola natalensis
Groottinktinkie

strong,
heavy bill

Length 15 cm **Weight** 25 g
Habitat Moist grassland with scattered bushes, especially around pans. Also forest clearings.
Habits Calls from a prominent perch.

Call
A range of loud, frog-like croaks and buzzes.

AT A GLANCE
✔ Strong, heavy bill
✔ Call

Similar-looking species None (heavy bill is distinctive)

Similar-sounding species None

NOTE See also breeding female (page 42) and non-breeding male (page 50).

Grey-backed Cisticola
(all except *C. s. windhoekensis* and *C. s. newtoni*)
Cisticola subruficapilla
Grysrugtinktinkie

bold back
markings

streaking
on chest or
flanks

Length 13 cm **Weight** 10 g
Habitat Fynbos and karoo.
Habits Frequently perches in the open.

Call (with comparative track)
A slow, bubbly rattle, occasionally with a few introductory *chuck* notes. Also a series of piercing whistles.

AT A GLANCE
✔ Streaking on chest or flanks
✔ Bold back markings
✔ Habitat
✔ Call

Similar-looking species None (the streaking on chest or flanks is distinctive)

Similar-sounding species Chirping (page 47), Tinkling (page 49) and Wailing (page 51) cisticolas

NOTE The streaking on the chest or flanks varies from bold to quite faint.

Wailing Cisticola
(C. l. lais, C. l. maculatis and
C. l. orebates)
Cisticola lais
Huiltinktinkie

Length 12 cm **Weight** 15 g
Habitat Montane grassy slopes with scattered
bushes and bracken.
Habits Perches in the open, frequently at the
top of a prominent bush.

Call (with comparative track)
A buzzy rattle, with one or two introductory
chuck notes. Also a series of piercing whistles.

Rattling Cisticola
(C. c. frater)
Cisticola chiniana
Bosveldtinktinkie

Length 15 cm **Weight** 15 g
Habitat Acacia woodland, patches of bush
in grassland and sometimes gardens.
Habits Conspicuous for a cisticola and easy
to find all year. Calls from the top of bushes
and trees.

Call
Harsh rattling sounds introduced by notes such
as *zee-zee-zee*, showing much variation.

Lazy Cisticola
(*C. a. aberrans*)
Cisticola aberrans
Luitinktinkie

indistinct back markings

thin bill

Length 14 cm **Weight** 14 g
Habitat Rocky areas with grass and scattered bushes; forest edges.
Habits Clambers about secretively, mouse-like. Cocks tail when calling.

Call
A shrill squeal, like a rubber toy being squeezed, mixed with buzzing and clicking notes.

AT A GLANCE
✔ Thin bill
✔ Indistinct back markings
✔ Habitat
✔ Call

 Similar-looking species Wailing Cisticola (*C. l. lais, C. l. maculatis* and *C. l. orebates*) and Rattling Cisticola (*C. c. frater*) (page 55)

 Similar-sounding species None

Typical habitats for this visual group

Mixed lowveld woodland is favoured by Croaking Cisticola.

Montane grassland with scattered trees is ideal for Wailing Cisticola.

Western Cape shrubland will often turn up a Grey-backed Cisticola.

STEP TWO – SEPARATING VISUAL GROUPS

Prinias & prinia-like warblers

The characteristic feature of all these small, energetic birds is the long tail, which they often raise and sometimes swivel from side to side. Prinias resemble typical warblers in some respects, but their rounder head shape and longer tail give them a distinctive and easily recognised profile. The upperparts are usually plain brown, but the underparts vary from plain to streaked, and some species (Rufous-eared Warbler and breeding Black-chested Prinia) are easily distinguished by their breast band.

Prinia calls are distinctive when compared to those of warblers and cisticolas, but this is not always a reliable feature, particularly in the case of the 'spotted' prinias. These species tend to be bolder and more conspicuous than typical warblers.

📷 LOOK FOR

- ✔ streaking on chest or throat
- ✔ throat colour
- ✔ eye colour
- ✔ presence of breast band
- ✔ colour of wash on underparts
- ✔ colour of wing panel
- ✔ distribution

PRINIAS CONSIST OF ONE VISUAL GROUP

Prinias & prinia-like warblers (page 58)

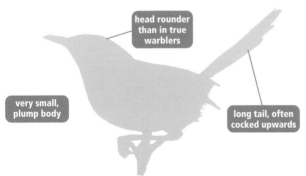

head rounder than in true warblers

very small, plump body

long tail, often cocked upwards

Black-chested Prinia

Tawny-flanked Prinia

Karoo Prinia

Drakensberg Prinia
Prinia hypoxantha
Drakensberglangstertjie

throat unstreaked

light streaking on yellowish chest and belly

Length 14 cm
Weight 10 g
Habitat Grass and
bushes along rivers,
on hillsides and at
forest edges.
Habits Found in
pairs or small groups. Moves from high altitude
to lower areas in winter.

Call (with comparative track)
Very similar *dzzzeeeep* to other prinias, but
with an excited introductory *pree-pree-pree*.
Very difficult to separate from Karoo Prinia on
call alone.

AT A GLANCE
✔ Light streaking on yellowish chest and
 belly
✔ Throat unstreaked
✔ Distribution

 Similar-looking species Karoo Prinia

Similar-sounding species Karoo,
Tawny-flanked (page 60) and
Black-chested (page 60) prinias

NOTE Juvenile Karoo Prinia looks very similar,
but the underparts are more sulphur-yellow
and the throat is streaked. There is a small
overlap with Karoo Prinia along the
Lesotho–KwaZulu-Natal border

Karoo Prinia
Prinia maculosa
Karoolangstertjie

streaking on throat and face

adult

heavy streaking on white to yellowish chest and belly

juvenile

Length 14 cm **Weight** 10 g
Habitat Varied shrublands and fynbos.
Habits Found in pairs or small groups. Calls from
a prominent perch, diving into the undergrowth
if it feels threatened.

Call (with comparative track)
Very similar *dzzzeeeep* to other prinias, but with
an excited introductory *pree-pree-pree*. Very
difficult to separate from Drakensberg Prinia on
call alone.

AT A GLANCE
✔ Heavy streaking on white to yellowish
 chest and belly
✔ Streaking on throat and face
✔ Distribution

 Similar-looking species Drakensberg
Prinia

Similar-sounding species Drakensberg,
Tawny-flanked (page 60) and
Black-chested (page 60) prinias

NOTE Drakensberg Prinia looks very similar
to juvenile Karoo Prinia, but the underparts
are less sulphur-yellow and the throat is
not streaked. There is a small overlap with
Drakensberg Prinia along the Lesotho–
KwaZulu-Natal border.

Namaqua Warbler
Phragmacia substriata
Namakwalangstertjie

light streaking on whitish chest

throat unstreaked

Roberts's Warbler
Oreophilais robertsi
Woudlangstertjie

plain grey head, lacks eyebrow

plain underparts, slightly mottled

Length 14 cm
Weight 12 g
Habitat Thick bush and reed beds near streams.
Habits Found singly or in pairs or small groups. Seldom emerges from the dense bush in which it forages, although sometimes feeds on the ground.

Length 14 cm **Weight** 9 g
Habitat Clearings in and edges of dense forest and bush.
Habits Found in pairs or small groups, sometimes in mixed bird parties.

Call
Reminiscent of the call of Green Wood-Hoopoe, but faster and higher pitched, like an excited laugh.

Call
A distinctive metallic *chi-chi-chi-chrrrrrrr*, reminiscent of the call of Little Swift.

AT A GLANCE

✔ Light streaking on whitish chest
✔ Throat unstreaked
✔ Distribution

Similar-looking species None (combination of dark eye and light streaking is distinctive)

Similar-sounding species None

NOTE Its range does not overlap with that of the similar Drakensberg Prinia.

AT A GLANCE

✔ Plain underparts, slightly mottled
✔ Plain grey head, lacks eyebrow
✔ Call

Similar-looking species None

Similar-sounding species None

Tawny-flanked Prinia
Prinia subflava
Bruinsylangstertjie

Length 12 cm **Weight** 9.5 g
Habitat Grass and bushes along streams and in clearings, avoiding dense forest.
Habits Found mainly in pairs. Forages in grass and bushes, often calling from within a bush.

Call (with comparative track)
A deliberate, piercing *chip chip chip* or a repeated *dzeep-dzeep-dzeep*, less buzzy than the call of Black-chested Prinia.

AT A GLANCE

✔ Plain underparts
✔ Obvious white eyebrow
✔ Call

 Similar-looking species Black-chested Prinia in non-breeding plumage

 Similar-sounding species Drakensberg (page 58), Karoo (page 58) and Black-chested prinias

NOTE Although the rufous wing panel is the most reliable feature, it becomes more difficult to see when the plumage is worn. The buff wash to the flanks, even when faded, together with a lack of a yellow wash to the underparts, is helpful. These birds are fairly vocal year round, which is helpful, as worn Tawny-flanked can strongly resemble some Black-chested Prinias.

Black-chested Prinia
(non-breeding)
Prinia flavicans
Swartbandlangstertjie

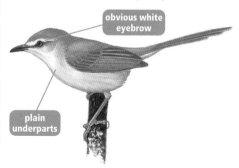

Length 14 cm **Weight** 9 g
Habitat Dry areas with bushes. Also drainage lines and croplands.
Habits Usually found in pairs. Perches higher on a bush than Tawny-flanked Prinia.

Call (with comparative track)
A series of *dzzzeeeep* and other notes, more buzzy than the call of Tawny-flanked Prinia.

AT A GLANCE

✔ Plain underparts
✔ Obvious white eyebrow
✔ Call

 Similar-looking species Tawny-flanked Prinia

 Similar-sounding species Drakensberg (page 58), Karoo (page 58) and Tawny-flanked prinias

NOTE A hint of a breast band from the breeding plumage is sometimes retained in winter. Tawny-flanked Prinia in worn plumage is similar but lacks the yellowish wash to the underparts. Subspecies *P. f. ortleppi* is more buff and very difficult to separate from Tawny-flanked. It is advisable with Black-chested and worn Tawny-flanked prinias to use call, as these birds are fairly vocal year round, which is always helpful.

STEP TWO – SEPARATING VISUAL GROUPS

Larks & sparrow-larks

Larks are, in general, ground-dwelling birds and, as a group, are sometimes confused with pipits, which are also terrestrial. However, a foraging lark moves slowly and pecks at the ground as it looks for seeds, whereas a pipit darts and runs as it hunts insects. Larks are also more robustly built than pipits and generally don't 'stand as tall'.

Lark plumage tends to be well marked and richly coloured, with a brown that is 'warmer' than a pipit's coloration. Variation in the colours of lark species depends to a certain extent on the soil colour of its habitat. There is variation, too, in bill shape, from small and conical to long and decurved, but lark bills are always more robust than the thin bills of pipits.

Bill shape is a defining feature when assigning larks to a visual group. Conical bills can be either small or stout, but they will always be short and symmetrical, with barely any curve. Long and decurved bills tend to look thinner, but that is only because of their length in relation to their width. Even the shortest bill in this group, belonging to the Spike-heeled Lark, is clearly long and curves down towards the tip. A third, or intermediate, group comprises larks with bills that are neither conical nor long and decurved. It includes the Rufous-naped Lark, for example, whose bill is shaped like that of the Karoo Thrush.

Belly colour is also an important determinant when assigning larks to a group and it helps to be able to recognise the base colour; even if there are streaks or spots on the belly, you will see that the background is either white or buffy. It is fairly easy to separate larks into six groups based on bill shape and belly colour.

When comparing the size of lark species, be aware that males and females can differ in weight by as much as 20 per cent and that this will be reflected in their build.

The calls of larks are reasonably distinctive and play a valuable role in species identification. Of special note is that Rufous-naped Lark has been included in several visual groups due to the complex and subjective nature of its back markings.

Short-clawed Lark

LOOK FOR

- ✔ bill shape
- ✔ belly colour
- ✔ markings on chest and/ or belly
- ✔ colour of bare parts
- ✔ coloration of and markings on wing
- ✔ distribution
- ✔ habitat
- ✔ call

Conical bill, white belly (page 63)

conical bill

white belly

Conical bill, belly not white (page 66)

conical bill

belly not white

Intermediate bill shape, belly not white, back scaled (page 68)

scaled back

bill neither conical nor long and decurved

belly not white

Intermediate bill shape, belly not white, back streaked or mottled (page 72)

back streaked or mottled

bill neither conical nor long and decurved

belly not white

Long, decurved bill (page 75)

long, decurved bill

Intermediate bill shape, white belly, no rufous wing panel (page 79)

shoulder patch does not contrast strongly with upperparts

bill neither conical nor long and decurved

no rufous wing panel

white belly

Striking plain rufous cap and shoulder patch (page 83)

striking rufous cap

striking rufous shoulder patch contrasts with white underparts

Intermediate bill shape, white belly, back not plain, rufous wing panel (page 84)

bill neither conical nor long and decurved

obvious rufous wing panel

white belly

Stark's Lark
Spizocorys starki
Woestynlewerik

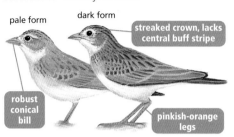

pale form
dark form
streaked crown, lacks central buff stripe
robust conical bill
pinkish-orange legs

Length 13 cm **Weight** 19 g
Habitat Flat arid and semi-arid land with sparse grass cover, often where the ground is stony.
Habits When not breeding, sometimes occurs in very large flocks on new-growth green grass.

Call
An over-excited version of the Cape Sparrow's morning call, with closely packed, sparrow-like chirps repeated in groups of two to five similar-sounding notes.

AT A GLANCE

✔ Pinkish-orange legs
✔ Robust conical bill
✔ Streaked crown, lacks central buff stripe
✔ Call

Similar-looking species None (the bill colour and breast band are distinctive)

Similar-sounding species None

NOTE Long feathers on the crown form a crest, which can be raised.

Gray's Lark
Ammomanopsis grayi
Namiblewerik

plain upperparts
A. g. grayi
A. g. hoeschi
grey legs
plain underparts

Length 14 cm **Weight** 21 g
Habitat Gravel soils with grasses and shrubs; absent from sand dunes and desert.
Habits Often in small groups. Does not flush easily.

Call (with comparative track)
A sequence of chirps similar to that of Pin-tailed Whydah, as well as a lower *foo-foo-foo*. Also a rising *soo-eeee* like Black-throated Canary, mixed with soft, high-pitched chirps.

AT A GLANCE

✔ Grey legs
✔ Plain underparts
✔ Plain upperparts

Similar-looking species None (the very plain upperparts are distinctive)

Similar-sounding species Pin-tailed Whydah (page 112); Black-throated Canary (page 142)

Rudd's Lark
Heteromirafra ruddi
Drakensbergewerik

crown has broad buff central stripe

robust conical bill

pinkish-orange legs

Length 14 cm
Weight 26 g
Habitat Upland grassland, usually on hilltops with short grass that is regularly burned.
Habits Easily overlooked unless singing. Has an upright stance.

Call ▮▮▮▮▮▮ ▮▮▮▮▮▮▮ ▮▮ ▮▮ ▮▮▮
A very nasal, buzzy *tzi-ri-ri-oo*. The rhythm and tone are quite distinctive.

Botha's Lark
Spizocorys fringillaris
Vaalrivierlewerik

short conical bill

pinkish-orange legs

streaked flanks

Length 14 cm
Weight 18 g
Habitat Heavily grazed short grass in upland grassland.
Habits In pairs or small groups. Well camouflaged, but white outer-tail feathers obvious when the tail fans out on take-off.

Call (with comparative track)
A buzzy, double-noted trill-whistle *chi-ree*, the first note being much shorter than the second, with barely a gap separating them. This is very rarely accompanied by any other sound.

▮▮▮▮▮▮ ▮▮ ▮▮▮▮▮ ▮▮▮▮ ▮▮

Pink-billed Lark
(*damarensis* race)
Spizocorys conirostris damarensis
Pienkbeklewerik

short conical bill

unstreaked flanks

pinkish-orange legs

Length 13 cm **Weight** 14 g
Habitat Ranges from burned grassland and freshly ploughed croplands to sports fields.
Habits Easily overlooked. Rarely perches in the open and runs across open ground from one patch of grass to another.

Call (with comparative track)
A double-noted trill, with both notes of equal length and a short but noticeable gap between them. Sometimes the call comprises three-noted trills interspersed with jumbled musical phrases.

▌▌▌▌▐▌ ▌ ▌▐▌▐▌▌▐▌▌▌ ▌▌ ▐▌▌

Black-eared Sparrow-Lark
(female)
Eremopterix australis
Swartoorlewerik

heavily streaked upperparts

extensive underpart streaking

grey legs

Length 13 cm
Weight 14 g
Habitat Arid karoo shrubland on red soils, and stony ground.
Habits In groups of up to 50 birds. Easily flushed and flies far when disturbed.

Call (with comparative track)
Similar to that of Little Bee-eater. Also chirps like those of Sclater's Lark but sparrow-like rather than reminiscent of European Bee-eater. Other, less dominant chirps are like those of House Sparrow.

▌▌▌▌▐▌ ▌▐▌▌▐▌▐▌▌▐▌ ▌ ▐▌▌

Chestnut-backed Sparrow-Lark (female)
Eremopterix leucotis
Rooiruglewerik

Grey-backed Sparrow-Lark (female)
Eremopterix verticalis
Grysruglewerik

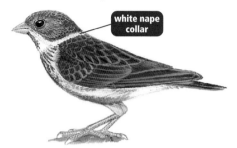

white nape collar

no nape collar

greyish back

greyish bill

Length 13 cm
Weight 22 g
Habitat Arid woodland and grassland, favouring burned areas and croplands; also sports fields.

Habits Usually in small groups, but also seen in large flocks. Circles an area when flushed.

Call (with comparative track)
A distinct high-pitched *pree-ree*. Also a continuous, weaver-like 'swizzling' interspersed with sparrow-like chirps.

Length 13 cm **Weight** 17 g
Habitat Arid grassland and karoo, favouring flat areas.
Habits Usually in small groups, but sometimes seen in large flocks at waterholes.

Call
Jumbled notes like those of white-eyes, each phrase ending with a distinctive, rising *pree-ree-oo*. Sometimes sounds quite agitated.

AT A GLANCE

✔ White nape collar
✔ Call

Similar-looking species None (the white nape collar is distinctive)

Similar-sounding species None

NOTE A dark belly patch places the female of this species in this group. In some individuals the collar does not extend all the way round the back of the neck and may not be visible from behind.

AT A GLANCE

✔ No nape collar
✔ Greyish bill
✔ Greyish back
✔ Call

Similar-looking species None (the combination of grey legs and grey back is distinctive)

Similar-sounding species None

NOTE A dark belly patch places the female of this species in this group.

Pink-billed Lark
(except *S. c. damarensis*)
Spizocorys conirostris
Pienkbeklewerik

Typical habitats for this visual group

no nape collar

brownish back, paler in western races

pink bill

Length 13 cm **Weight** 14 g
Habitat Ranges from burned grassland and freshly ploughed croplands to sports fields.
Habits Easily overlooked. Rarely perches in the open and runs across open ground from one patch of grass to another.

Call (with comparative track)
A double-noted trill, with both notes of equal length and a short but noticeable gap between them. Sometimes the call comprises three-noted trills interspersed with jumbled musical phrases.

AT A GLANCE

✔ No nape collar
✔ Pink bill
✔ Brownish back, paler in western races

 Similar-looking species None (the pink bill is distinctive)

 Similar-sounding species Botha's (page 64) and Red-capped (page 83) larks

NOTE No range overlap between the pale-bellied race and the similar Botha's Lark.

The species in this group can be found on burned land (top), sports fields (middle) and ploughed croplands (above), although Grey-backed Sparrow-Lark is unlikely to be found on sports fields.

Eastern Clapper Lark
(all except *M. f. damarensis*)
Mirafra fasciolata
Hoëveldklappertjie

short, stout bill

Length 15 cm **Weight** 30 g
Habitat Tall grassland, either open or with scattered bushes.
Habits Difficult to flush; when disturbed, prefers to run but may perch in open.

Call (with comparative track)
A wing rattle of constant speed culminating in an ascending, drawn-out whistle, given as the bird flies upward in display and then drops back to the ground.

Cape Clapper Lark
Mirafra apiata
Kaapse Klappertjie

short, stout bill

M. a. apiata

M. a. marjoriae (extreme southern distribution)

Length 13 cm **Weight** 28 g
Habitat Dense bush and fynbos. Sometimes in cropland near suitable habitat.
Habits Difficult to flush; when flushed, prefers to run but may perch in open before dropping down into denser vegetation.

Call (with comparative track)
An accelerating wing rattle that culminates in an ascending or floaty whistle, given during the display flight.

AT A GLANCE

✔ Short, stout bill
✔ Distribution
✔ Call

 Similar-looking species All in this visual group. Rufous-naped (page 69) is larger with a heavier bill. When not calling, Rufous-naped is best separated by build and bill size, with all the others looking like short, stubby Rufous-naped Larks.

 Similar-sounding species Cape Clapper Lark; Flappet Lark (pages 69, 70)

NOTE Distribution plays an important role in separating clapper larks.

AT A GLANCE

✔ Short, stout bill
✔ Distribution
✔ Call

 Similar-looking species All in this visual group. Rufous-naped (page 69) is larger with a heavier bill. When not calling, Rufous-naped is best separated by build and bill size, with all the others looking like short, stubby Rufous-naped Larks.

 Similar-sounding species Eastern Clapper Lark; Flappet Lark (pages 69, 70)

NOTE Distribution plays an important role when separating clapper larks.

Flappet Lark

(all except *M. r. smithersi*)
Mirafra rufocinnamomea
Laeveldklappertjie

short, stout bill

Length 14 cm **Weight** 26 g
Habitat Grassy clearings and gravel roads in mostly broad-leaved but also acacia woodland.
Habits Remains hidden when not displaying, and difficult to flush. In display flight, male claps wings together to produce a rattling sound.

Call (with comparative track)
One or two short wing rattles followed by a longer one. In ideal conditions, a soft jumbled phrase can be heard at the end of the rattle (in the clapper larks, a piercing whistle concludes the rattle).

AT A GLANCE

✔ Short, stout bill
✔ Distribution
✔ Call

 Similar-looking species All in this visual group. Rufous-naped is larger with a heavier bill.

 Similar-sounding species Eastern and Cape clapper larks (pages 68, 70)

NOTE Visually similar to the clapper larks, but habitat and call help to separate them. Birds tend to be darkest towards the east of their distribution

---

Rufous-naped Lark

(all except *M. a. pallida*)
Mirafra africana
Rooineklewerik

large, heavy bill

large, bulky size

Length 17 cm **Weight** 42 g
Habitat Ranges from grassland to woodland, with the exception of dense grassland.
Habits Inconspicuous in winter, but sings prominently from perches in summer. Difficult to flush.

Call
Distinctive but highly variable, comprising three or four piercing whistles such as *tri-lee-tri-loo* or *tree-ri-loo*. Sometimes also a wing rattle.

AT A GLANCE

✔ Large, heavy bill
✔ Large, bulky size
✔ Call

 Similar-looking species All in this visual group. Rufous-naped is larger with a heavier bill. When not calling, Rufous-naped is best separated by build and bill size, with all the others looking like short, stubby Rufous-naped Larks.

 Similar-sounding species None

NOTE Crown more richly coloured than nape, giving a capped appearance.

Separating Rufous-naped, Flappet and Clapper larks

This group of LBJs is one of the most challenging to identify with confidence. Eastern and Cape Clapper, and Flappet larks have long been considered a tricky trio. We have added Rufous-naped Lark, which can sometimes be confused with any one of these three.

Markings on the upperparts are often quoted as a means of separating these species, but it is not the most reliable identifying feature, as they all may have barring or scaling. The best way to separate these birds is by their calls, but when they are not calling, body size, build and bill size are useful identifying features.

Eastern Clapper
Smaller size with stout build
15 cm 30 g

more uniform crown and nape

small, stout bill

Cape Clapper
Smaller size with stout build
13 cm 28 g

more uniform crown and nape

small, stout bill

Flappet
Smaller size with stout build
14 cm 26 g

more uniform crown and nape

small, stout bill

Rufous-naped
Large size and more elongated build
17 cm 42 g

richer, darker crown (crest often not raised) and paler nape

large, heavy bill

If you establish that the bird is a Clapper or Flappet lark, the best way to distinguish between them will be habitat and distribution.

Clapper larks are grassland species and will always be found in that habitat. Flappet Lark is more regularly found in broad-leaved woodland savanna. Where Flappet Lark does occur in coastal grassland, Eastern Clapper does not.

CALL	SONOGRAM
A wing rattle of constant speed culminating in an ascending, drawn-out whistle, given as the bird flies upward in display and then drops back to the ground.	
Accelerating wing clapping with a rising whistle that starts near the end of the rattle.	
A short rattle followed by a long rattle, which is often followed by much softer but clear whistling including some mimicry.	
A highly varied but recognisable series of whistled *tri-lee-tri-loo*.	

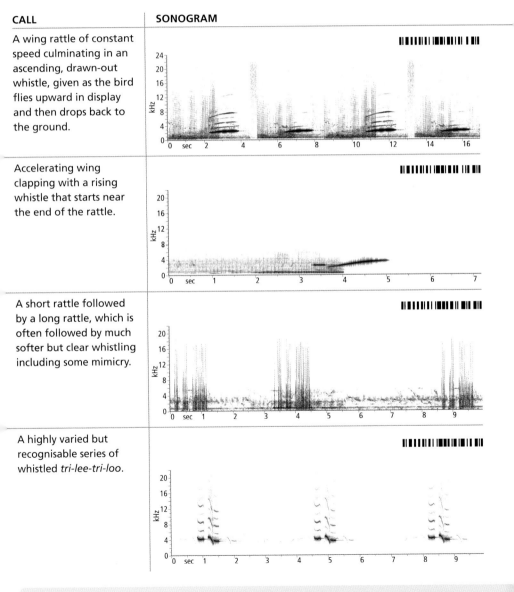

Melodious Lark
Mirafra cheniana
Spotlewerik

rufous edges to primaries

short bill

bold, dark streaking restricted to chest

Sabota Lark (all except
C. s. waibeli, sabotoides and *naevia*)
Calendulauda sabota
Sabotalewerik

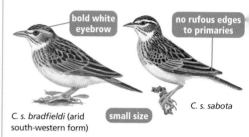

bold white eyebrow

no rufous edges to primaries

C. s. bradfieldi (arid south-western form)

small size

C. s. sabota

Length 12 cm **Weight** 20 g
Habitat Rooigras-dominated grassland, where grass is short and patchy.
Habits Inconspicuous unless singing, which it usually does in flight. Difficult to flush.

Call (with comparative track)
A continuous stream of musical notes and mimicry with very short gaps between phrases. Similar to that of Sabota Lark but lacks the piercing introductory notes. Some calls have a three- or four-noted phrase structure similar to that of reed-warblers.

Length 14 cm **Weight** 25 g
Habitat Open acacia woodland to Karoo scrub, where it occurs among larger bushes.
Habits Often perches, usually on a nearby bush when flushed.

Call (with comparative track)
Short phrases with some mimicry, usually with piercing introductory notes that have an easily recognisable tone. Similar to the call of Melodious Lark but with longer pauses between phrases.

 ✔ Rufous edges to primaries
✔ Short bill
✔ Bold, dark streaking restricted to chest

 Similar-looking species None (the rufous edges to the wing panel and short bill are distinctive)

Similar-sounding species Sabota Lark

Note Separated from Rufous-naped Lark (page 74) by smaller size, shorter bill and streaking more restricted to chest. It also lacks the rich rufous nape patch. Has a heavier bill and heavier chest streaking than Fawn-coloured Lark (page 74).

✔ No rufous edges to primaries
✔ Small size
✔ Bold white eyebrow

 Similar-looking species None

 Similar-sounding species Melodious Lark

Sclater's Lark
Spizocorys sclateri
Namakwalewerik

buff eyebrow

no rufous edges to primaries

small size

Length 13 cm **Weight** 20 g
Habitat Arid areas with small bushes, usually on quartzitic soil.
Habits Walks slowly when foraging. Inconspicuous except at water, where it occurs in large groups.

Call (with comparative track)
Jumbled, with *purp* notes like those of a European Bee-eater, and short chirps intermediate between those of a warbler and a sparrow.

AT A GLANCE

✔ No rufous edges to primaries
✔ Small size
✔ Buff eyebrow

Similar-looking species None

Similar-sounding species Tractrac Chat (page 99)

NOTE This species also has a heavy and distinctive, almost upward-pointing bill that may cause confusion with Large-billed Lark.

Large-billed Lark
Galerida magnirostris
Dikbeklewerik

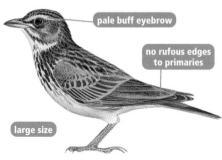

pale buff eyebrow

no rufous edges to primaries

large size

Length 18 cm **Weight** 43 g
Habitat Arid areas, from fynbos to dry grassland.
Habits Walks slowly when foraging. Sometimes occurs in groups of up to 25 birds. Flies some distance when flushed, but easily located when vocal.

Call
In two parts: a single-noted click followed by a full, fluty and almost comical jumbled whistle.

AT A GLANCE

✔ No rufous edges to primaries
✔ Large size
✔ Pale buff eyebrow

Similar-looking species None

Similar-sounding species Karoo (page 80), Barlow's (page 80), Red (page 81) and Dune (page 81) larks

NOTE Be aware that the large size and heavy bill of Rufous-naped Lark (page 74) may cause confusion with this species.

Rufous-naped Lark
(*M. a. pallida*)
Mirafra africana
Rooineklewerik

rufous edges to primaries

large bill

bold, dark chest streaking extending to upper belly

Length 17 cm
Weight 42 g
Habitat Ranges from grassland to woodland, with the exception of dense grassland.
Habits Inconspicuous in winter, but sings prominently from perches in summer. Difficult to flush.

Call
Distinctive but highly variable, comprising three or four piercing whistles such as *tri-lee-tri-loo* or *tree-ri-loo*. Sometimes also a wing rattle.

AT A GLANCE
✔ Rufous edges to primaries
✔ Large bill
✔ Bold, dark chest streaking extending to upper belly
✔ Call

 Similar-looking species Eastern Clapper Lark (page 68)

 Similar-sounding species None

NOTE Crown more richly coloured than nape, giving a capped appearance when viewed from behind. This, with larger size, heavy bill and more extensive chest streaking, separates it from Melodious (page 72) and Fawn-coloured (*C. a. harei*) larks.

Fawn-coloured Lark
(*C. a. harei*)
Calendulauda africanoides
Vaalbruinlewerik

rufous edges to primaries

short bill

thin, fine streaks restricted to chest

Length 15 cm
Weight 23 g
Habitat A range of woodland, particularly on sandy soils and extending to dune habitats in the Northern Cape.
Habits Walks in open patches between grass tufts and bushes. Male calls from a perch.

Call
Includes a jumbled twittering phrase that speeds up across the call. Very similar to that of Cape Grassbird but flutier and less harsh.

AT A GLANCE
✔ Rufous edges to primaries
✔ Short bill
✔ Thin, fine streaks restricted to chest
✔ Call

 Similar-looking species Finer billed with finer chest streaking than Melodious Lark (page 72). Also smaller size bill than Rufous-naped Lark (pages 69, 74, 85)

 Similar-sounding species None

NOTE The contrast between the sandy upperparts and the white underparts is more striking than in other members of this group. May resemble pale-bellied Rufous-naped Lark, but is smaller, with smaller bill, and uniformly coloured crown and nape.

Typical habitats for this visual group

Karoo scrub is the habitat of all of the species in this group, except Eastern Long-billed and Short-clawed larks.

Grassland with scattered bushes in the dry North West province is the ideal habitat for the Short-clawed Lark.

Eastern Long-billed Lark
Certhilauda semitorquata
Grasveldlangbeklewerik

long tail

Length 18 cm
Weight 40 g
Habitat Grassland in hilly areas, particularly in short grass on stony ground.
Habits Forages mainly alone or in pairs.

Call (with comparative track)
A piercing descending whistle, given either when perched or in display flight.

AT A GLANCE

✔ Long tail
✔ Habitat
✔ Distribution

 Similar-looking species Cape (page 76), Agulhas (page 76), Karoo (page 77) and Benguela (page 77) long-billed larks; Short-clawed Lark (page 78)

 Similar-sounding species Cape (page 76), Agulhas (page 76), Karoo (page 77) and Benguela (page 77) long-billed larks; Short-clawed Lark (page 78)

NOTE Distribution is crucial for identification as plumage coloration depends on the colour of the local soil.

Cape Long-billed Lark
Certhilauda curvirostris
Weskuslangbeklewerik

long tail

Length 22 cm **Weight** 60 g
Habitat Coastal scrub and old farmlands with patchy vegetation.
Habits Forages mainly alone or in pairs.

Call (with comparative track)
A piercing descending whistle given either when perched or in display flight.

|||||||||| |||||||| ||| |||

Agulhas Long-billed Lark
Certhilauda brevirostris
Overberglangbeklewerik

long tail

Length 19 cm
Weight 45 g
Habitat Short grassland and old farmland with short grass, mainly on stony ground.
Habits Forages mainly alone or in pairs.

Call (with comparative track)
A piercing whistle rising and falling in two parts, given either when perched or in display flight.

|||||||| |||||||||||| |||

AT A GLANCE

✔ Long tail
✔ Habitat
✔ Distribution

 Similar-looking species Eastern (page 75), Agulhas, Karoo (page 77) and Benguela (page 77) long-billed larks; Short-clawed Lark (page 78)

 Similar-sounding species Eastern (page 75), Agulhas, Karoo (page 77) and Benguela (page 77) long-billed larks; Short-clawed Lark (page 78)

NOTE Distribution is crucial for identification as plumage coloration depends on the colour of the local soil.

AT A GLANCE

✔ Long tail
✔ Habitat
✔ Distribution

 Similar-looking species Eastern (page 75), Cape, Karoo (page 77) and Benguela (page 77) long-billed larks; Short-clawed Lark (page 78)

 Similar-sounding species Eastern (page 75), Cape, Karoo (page 77) and Benguela (page 77) long-billed larks; Short-clawed Lark (page 78)

NOTE Distribution is crucial for identification as plumage coloration depends on the colour of the local soil.

Karoo Long-billed Lark
Certhilauda subcoronata
Karoolangbeklewerik

long tail

Length 20 cm **Weight** 40 g
Habitat Karoo scrub on stony ground, particularly on reddish soils.
Habits Forages mainly alone or in pairs.

Call (with comparative track)
A piercing descending whistle, given either when perched or in display flight.

AT A GLANCE

✔ Long tail
✔ Habitat
✔ Distribution

Similar-looking species Eastern (page 75), Cape (page 76), Agulhas (page 76), and Benguela long-billed larks; Short-clawed Lark (page 78)

Similar-sounding species Eastern (page 75), Cape (page 76), Agulhas (page 76), and Benguela long-billed larks; Short-clawed Lark (page 78)

NOTE Distribution is crucial for identification as plumage coloration depends on the colour of the local soil.

Benguela Long-billed Lark
Certhilauda benguelensis
Kaokolangbeklewerik

long tail

Length 19 cm **Weight** 50 g
Habitat Arid scrub on stony ground.
Habits Forages mainly alone or in pairs.

Call (with comparative track)
A piercing descending whistle, given either when perched or in display flight.

AT A GLANCE

✔ Long tail
✔ Habitat
✔ Distribution

Similar-looking species Eastern (page 75), Cape (page 76), Agulhas (page 76), and Karoo long-billed larks; Short-clawed Lark (page 78)

Similar-sounding species Eastern (page 75), Cape (page 76), Agulhas (page 76) and Karoo long-billed larks; Short-clawed Lark (page 78)

NOTE Distribution is crucial for identification as plumage coloration depends on the colour of the local soil.

Short-clawed Lark
Certhilauda chuana
Kortkloulewerik

long tail

Length 19 cm **Weight** 35 g
Habitat Grassland with scattered small bushes.
Habits Runs in short bursts, like a pipit.

Call (with comparative track)
A piercing fluty whistle, similar in tone to a person whistling, given either when perched or in display flight. Also a series of whistles and liquid trills similar to those of a rock thrush.

AT A GLANCE

✔ Long tail
✔ Habitat
✔ Distribution
✔ Call

 Similar-looking species Eastern (page 75), Cape (page 76), Agulhas (page 76), Karoo (page 77) and Benguela (page 77) long-billed larks

 Similar-sounding species Eastern (page 75), Cape (page 76), Agulhas (page 76), Karoo (page 77) and Benguela (page 77) long-billed larks

NOTE Among long-billed larks, the distribution of Eastern Long-billed Lark is the only one to overlap with that of this species. Differences in habitat and call will help to distinguish between them.

Spike-heeled Lark
Chersomanes albofasciata
Vlaktelewerik

white tips to tail (when visible)

short tail

Length 14 cm
Weight 25 g
Habitat Patchy grassland to Karoo scrub, where vegetation is sparse.
Habits Usually in smallish groups. Runs at a crouch when disturbed.

Call
A rapid series of soft chuckling sounds, very low in volume, similar to that of Green Wood-Hoopoe.

AT A GLANCE

✔ Short tail
✔ White tips to tail (when visible)
✔ Call

 Similar-looking species None (the short, white-tipped tail is distinctive)

 Similar-sounding species None

NOTE Back colour varies from rufous to grey in different races. The white tips to the tail can be difficult to see, especially when the bird is perched or on the ground, but the short tail is diagnostic within this group.

Dusky Lark
Pinarocorys nigricans
Donkerlewerik

heavily scaled slate-grey back

Length 20 cm
Weight 39 g
Habitat Dry savanna and broad-leaved woodland, particularly along gravel roads and around cattle and game.
Habits Often solitary or in small groups. When walking, stops, flicks wings and continues.

Call
A shrill *preeea*, similar to a referee's whistle, but this is seldom heard in southern Africa. When here, the birds generally give soft, less diagnostic calls.

Sabota Lark (*C.s. waibeli, sabotoides* and *naevia*)
Calendulauda sabota
Sabotalewerik

brownish back, streaked dark

Length 14 cm **Weight** 25 g
Habitat Open acacia woodland to Karoo scrub, where it occurs among larger bushes.
Habits Often perches, usually on a nearby bush when flushed.

Call (with comparative track)
Short phrases with some mimicry, usually with piercing introductory notes that have an easily recognisable tone. Similar to the call of Melodious Lark but with longer pauses between phrases.

Karoo Lark
Calendulauda albescens
Karoolewerik

Barlow's Lark
Calendulauda barlowi
Barlowse Lewerik

streaked flanks

unstreaked flanks

Length 17 cm
Weight 28 g
Habitat Coastal and arid scrub, usually on soft soils or stony ground.
Habits In pairs, defending territory year round. When disturbed, either runs away or gives alarm call from a perch.

Call (with comparative track)
A more varied range of *chip* notes than in Dune Lark or Barlow's Lark, and a longer and more complex, swallow-like gurgle.

Length 18 cm **Weight** 29 g
Habitat Sparsely vegetated shrubland and grassy dunes; often associated with euphorbia succulents.
Habits In pairs. Most active in early morning, sheltering in shade during the day.

Call (with comparative track)
A series of 6–9 *chip* notes followed by a swallow-like trill (the shortest within the group).

AT A GLANCE

 ✔ Habitat
✔ Distribution
 ✔ Streaked flanks

🔭 **Similar-looking species** None (the heavy streaking on the flanks is distinctive)

🐦 **Similar-sounding species** Large-billed (page 73), Barlow's, Red (page 81) and Dune (page 81) larks

NOTE The ranges of this species and Barlow's Lark overlap near Port Nolloth, where some hybridisation does occur. Races vary in colour from rich brown to grey.

AT A GLANCE

 ✔ Habitat
✔ Distribution
 ✔ Unstreaked flanks

🔭 **Similar-looking species** Karoo, Red (page 81) and Dune (page 81) larks

🐦 **Similar-sounding species** Large-billed (page 73), Karoo, Red (page 81) and Dune (page 81) larks

NOTE The ranges of this species and Karoo Lark overlap near Port Nolloth, where some hybridisation does occur. Birds in the north are plain above, resembling Dune Lark.

Red Lark
Calendulauda burra
Rooilewerik

Dune Lark
Calendulauda erythrochlamys
Duinlewerik

plumage colour variable

unstreaked flanks

unstreaked flanks

Length 19 cm **Weight** 37 g
Habitat Dunes with grass cover.
Habits Usually in pairs. Runs between grass patches or flies to a perch when disturbed. Calls most often in the early morning.

Call (with comparative track)
One of the longest and most complex in the group, starting with a series of rattles followed by a fast jumbled phrase and ending with a gurgled warble.

Length 17 cm **Weight** 28 g
Habitat Namib dunes with grasses.
Habits Usually in small groups. Runs across open ground between patches of grass.

Call (with comparative track)
The softest, thinnest and longest in the group. Eight or more widowbird-like chirps followed by a soft, swallow-like gurgle.

AT A GLANCE

✔ Habitat
✔ Distribution
✔ Unstreaked flanks

 Similar-looking species Karoo (page 80), Barlow's (page 80) and Dune larks

 Similar-sounding species Large-billed (page 73), Karoo (page 80), Barlow's (page 80) and Dune larks

Note Although the red of the upperparts may extend onto the shoulder, this species lacks the striking plain rufous cap and contrasting shoulder patch of Red-capped Lark.

AT A GLANCE

✔ Habitat
✔ Distribution
✔ Unstreaked flanks

 Similar-looking species Barlow's (page 80) and Red larks, but the faint breast streaking should distinguish it.

 Similar-sounding species Large-billed (page 73), Karoo (page 80), Barlow's (page 80) and Red larks

The Karoo Lark Complex

The four species in the **Karoo Lark Complex** – Dune, Red, Karoo and Barlow larks – are restricted to the more arid regions of southern Africa. They are all very similar in appearance and behaviour, and are particularly difficult to separate on plumage. Although they share the same broad habitat, each has slightly different habitat requirements and this affects their individual ranges, so there is not a lot of overlap in their distribution (see map). The simplest way to separate them, therefore, is on distribution.

There is no overlap in the ranges of Dune and Red larks; their ranges can be used as a fairly reliable distinguishing feature. Where Karoo and Red larks overlap, the Karoo Lark can be distinguished by the streaking all the way down the flanks. In Namibia, Dune Lark occurs north of Lüderitz and Barlow's Lark to the south. There is no known overlap of the two species, but care must be taken as Barlow's becomes paler and more like Dune the further

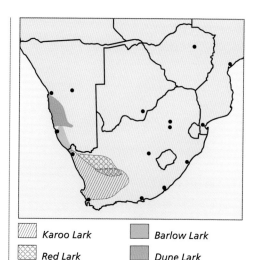

▨ Karoo Lark	▨ Barlow Lark
▨ Red Lark	▨ Dune Lark

north you go. The trickiest birds in this group occur just south of Port Nolloth, where Karoo and Barlow's larks hybridise. These hybrid birds have partial streaking down the flanks, whereas Karoo Lark has streaks all the way down the flanks and Barlow's shows none at all.

Karoo Lark

streaked flanks

Barlow's Lark

unstreaked flanks

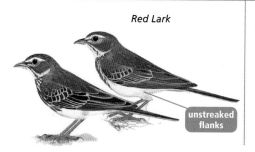

Red Lark

unstreaked flanks

Dune Lark

unstreaked flanks

Red-capped Lark
Calandrella cinerea
Rooikoplewerik

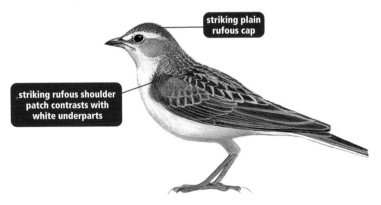

striking plain rufous cap

striking rufous shoulder patch contrasts with white underparts

Length 15 cm **Weight** 24 g

Habitat A range of grassland habitats, but most regularly in ploughed and burned fields.

Habits Forages in large groups. May raise crest when alarmed.

Call (with comparative track)
A jumble of phrases, the most characteristic being a descending whistle comprising two notes very close together, with a trill on the second note. Mimicry is often included, especially during the high display flight.

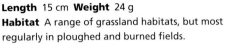

AT A GLANCE

✔ Striking plain rufous cap
✔ Striking rufous shoulder patch contrasts with white underparts

Similar-looking species None, although the juvenile resembles Sclater's Lark (page 73)

Similar-sounding species Botha's (page 64) and Pink-billed (page 67) larks

NOTE With its brown cap and shoulder and 'tear drop' below the eye, the juvenile resembles Sclater's Lark.

Eastern Clapper Lark
(*M. f. damarensis*)
Mirafra fasciolata
Hoëveldklappertjie

boldly streaked chest

boldly patterned scapulars and greater coverts

Length 15 cm **Weight** 30 g
Habitat Tall grassland, either open or with scattered bushes.
Habits Difficult to flush; when disturbed, prefers to run but may perch in open.

Call (with comparative track)
A wing rattle of constant speed culminating in an ascending, drawn-out whistle, given as the bird flies upward in display and then drops back to the ground.

‖‖‖‖‖‖‖‖ ‖‖‖‖‖‖‖ ‖ ‖‖‖

AT A GLANCE

✔ Boldly streaked chest
✔ Boldly patterned scapulars and greater coverts
✔ (See Clapper, Flappet, Rufous-naped larks pages 68 and 69)
✔ Call

Similar-looking species All in this visual group.

Similar-sounding species Cape Clapper Lark (pages 68, 70); Flappet Lark (page 69, 70)

NOTE Distribution plays an important role in separating clapper larks. Rufous-naped Lark is larger with a heavier bill. When not calling, they are best separated by build and bill size, with all the others in this group looking like short, stubby Rufous-naped Larks. Fawn-coloured and Monotonous larks are not as intricately marked on the back.

Flappet Lark (*M. r. smithersi*)
Mirafra rufocinnamomea
Laeveldklappertjie

boldly patterned scapulars and greater coverts

boldly streaked chest

Length 14 cm **Weight** 26 g
Habitat Grassy clearings and gravel roads in mostly broad-leaved but also acacia woodland.
Habits Remains hidden when not displaying, and difficult to flush. In display flight, male claps wings together to produce a rattling sound.

Call (with comparative track)
One or two short wing rattles followed by a longer one. In ideal conditions, a soft jumbled phrase can be heard at the end of the rattle (in the clapper larks, a piercing whistle concludes the rattle).

‖‖‖‖‖‖‖ ‖‖‖‖‖‖ ‖‖ ‖‖‖

AT A GLANCE

✔ Boldly streaked chest
✔ Boldly patterned scapulars and greater coverts
✔ (See Clapper, Flappet, Rufous-naped larks page 68 and 69)
✔ Call

Similar-looking species All in this visual group

Similar-sounding species Eastern and Cape clapper larks (pages 68, 70)

NOTE Visually similar to the clapper larks, but habitat and call help to separate them. Birds tend to be darkest towards the east of their distribution. Rufous-naped is larger with a heavier bill. When not calling, they are best separated by build and bill size, with all the others in this group looking like short, stubby Rufous-naped Larks. Fawn-coloured and Monotonous larks are not as intricately marked on the back.

Rufous-naped Lark
(*M. a. pallida*)
Mirafra africana
Rooineklewerik

scapulars and greater coverts with indistinct to bold barring

boldly streaked chest

Length 17 cm **Weight** 42 g
Habitat Ranges from grassland to woodland, with the exception of dense grassland.
Habits Inconspicuous in winter, but sings prominently from perches in summer. Difficult to flush.

Call
Distinctive but highly variable, comprising three or four piercing whistles such as *tri-lee-tri-loo or tree-ri-loo*. Sometimes also a wing rattle.

AT A GLANCE

✔ Boldly streaked chest
✔ Scapulars and greater coverts with indistinct to bold barring
✔ (See Clapper, Flappet, Rufous-naped larks pages 68 and 69)
✔ Call

Similar-looking species All in this visual group

Similar-sounding species None

NOTE Crown more richly coloured than nape, giving a capped appearance. When not calling, they are best separated by build and bill size, with all the others in this group looking like short, stubby Rufous-naped Larks. Fawn-coloured and Monotonous larks are not as intricately marked on the back.

Fawn-coloured Lark
(all except *C. a. harei*)
Calendulauda africanoides
Vaalbruinlewerik

scapular and greater coverts lack barring; finely streaked back

fine to indistinctly streaked chest

Length 15 cm **Weight** 23 g
Habitat A range of woodland, particularly on sandy soils and extending to dune habitats in the Northern Cape.
Habits Walks in open patches between grass tufts and bushes. Male calls from a perch.

Call
Includes a jumbled twittering phrase that speeds up across the call. Very similar to that of Cape Grassbird but flutier and less harsh.

AT A GLANCE

✔ Fine to indistinctly streaked chest
✔ Scapular and greater coverts lack barring
✔ Finely streaked back
✔ Call

Similar-looking species All in this visual group

Similar-sounding species None

NOTE The contrast between the sandy upperparts and the white underparts is more striking than in other members of this group. May resemble pale-bellied Rufous-Naped Lark, but is smaller, with smaller bill, and uniformly coloured crown and nape. This species is not as intricately patterned on the back as Rufous-naped and the clapper larks.

Monotonous Lark
Mirafra passerina
Bosveldlewerik

scapular and greater coverts indistinctly barred

boldly mottled back

boldly streaked chest

Length 14 cm **Weight** 24 g
Habitat A range of woodland, avoiding arid areas.
Habits Reclusive and silent, and thus difficult to locate when not breeding.

Call
Liquid, bubbly and rhythmical, with some phrases similar to those of a bee-eater call and others more like that of a Cinnamon-breasted Bunting. Repeats the same phrase monotonously.

AT A GLANCE

✔ Boldly streaked chest
✔ Scapular and greater coverts indistinctly barred
✔ Boldly mottled back
✔ Call

 Similar-looking species None (the buff breast band and white throat are distinctive)

 Similar-sounding species None

Typical habitats for this visual group

Flappet Lark is predominantly found in broad-leaved woodland.

Woodland on sandy soils is the ideal habitat for Fawn-coloured Lark.

Eastern Clapper Lark favours open grassland.

Flycatchers

The grey-brown flycatchers are small, dull birds with very few distinctive markings. The presence of rictal bristles (whiskers at the base of the bill) separates flycatchers from other LBJ families, notably chats, but the bristles are often difficult to see. The plain tail of birds in this family is more reliable as a distinguishing feature from wheatears, chats and honeyguides, all of which have a striking tail pattern and sometimes also a rump that is colourful or clearly marked. Noticeably short legs are another flycatcher characteristic, and, even though the legs of the Chat Flycatcher are somewhat longer, they are still shorter than those of regular chats.

Flycatcher calls are simple, comprising scratchy notes and soft whistles.

The birds are often seen on a prominent, relatively low and usually covered perch, from which they hawk insects in flight or, like the Marico, Pale and Chat flycatchers, take them on the ground before returning to their original position. Their motionless, upright stance while perched contrasts with the more horizontal feeding posture of chats and wheatears.

LOOK FOR

- ✔ overall grey-brown coloration
- ✔ head markings
- ✔ underpart coloration and presence or absence of streaking on chest
- ✔ plain tail
- ✔ hawking behaviour

FLYCATCHERS HAVE ONLY ONE VISUAL GROUP

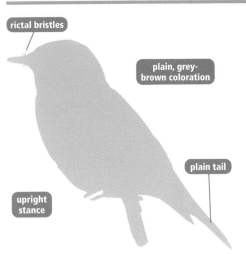

rictal bristles

plain, grey-brown coloration

plain tail

upright stance

Spotted Flycatcher

Typical habitats for this visual group

Open woodland, particularly with a clear understorey (such as camp and picnic sites), is ideal for the Spotted Flycatcher.

Sparsely covered grassland in the drier west of the region is a good place to search for the rather bulky Chat Flycatcher.

The Marico Flycatcher is one of the more common species found in acacia woodland, although Spotted and Pale flycatchers may also occur here.

Chat Flycatcher
Bradornis infuscatus
Grootvlieëvanger

large size (same size as a thrush)

pale throat

warm, soft brown wash to underparts

Length 20 cm **Weight** 37 g
Habitat Open woodland to sparsely covered grassland.
Habits Solitary or in pairs, occasionally in small groups. Hawks insects from a perch, taking large portions of its food from the ground.

Call (with comparative track)
A series of warbler-like notes, similar to the soft clucks of the Helmeted Guineafowl. Also a series of rapidly repeated, sparrow-like *chirrup* sounds.

AT A GLANCE
✔ Warm, soft brown wash to underparts
✔ Pale throat
✔ Same size as a thrush

 Similar-looking species Pale Flycatcher (page 89)

 Similar-sounding species Pale Flycatcher (page 89)

NOTE Juveniles are streaked only on the chest and flanks. The flight feathers of juveniles and adults have buff edges.

Marico Flycatcher
Bradornis mariquensis
Maricovlieëvanger

rich sandy brown upperparts

contrasting pale underparts

smaller than a thrush

Length 18 cm **Weight** 24 g
Habitat Drier areas
with acacia woodland
and savanna.
Habits Solitary or in
pairs, sometimes in
small groups. Hawks
insects from a perch,
taking large portions
of its food from the
ground.

Call ▌▌▌▌▌▌ ▌▌▌▌▌▌▌▌▌▌ ▌▌▌
Similar to that of the House Sparrow but
including some high-pitched, typical flycatcher
tseeep notes.

Pale Flycatcher
Bradornis pallidus
Muiskleurvlieëvanger

grey-brown upperparts

smaller than a thrush

off-white underparts (dirty looking)

Length 16 cm **Weight** 22 g
Habitat Forest, acacia and miombo woodland
and bushveld.
Habits Solitary or in pairs. Territorial. Hawks
insects from a perch, taking large portions of its
food from the ground. Flicks tail when landing.

Call (with comparative track)
A series of excited, weaver-like 'swizzling'
sounds, similar to those of the Village Weaver.
▌▌▌▌▌▌ ▌▌▌▌▌▌▌▌▌ ▌▌▌

Spotted Flycatcher
Muscicapa striata
Europese Vlieëvanger

heavily streaked forehead

tiny size

no streaking on belly

African Dusky Flycatcher
Muscicapa adusta
Donkervlieëvanger

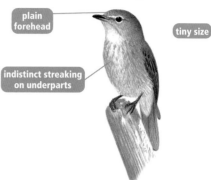

plain forehead

tiny size

indistinct streaking on underparts

Length 14 cm
Weight 15 g
Habitat Woodland and gardens where the understorey is open.
Habits Solitary or sometimes in pairs. Hawks insects from a perch.

Call (with comparative track)
A sharp *tsee-chik* and a very high-pitched, short but descending *tseeee*.

AT A GLANCE

✔ Heavily streaked forehead
✔ No streaking on belly
✔ Tiny size

Similar-looking species None (the streaking on the head is distinctive)

Similar-sounding species African Dusky Flycatcher

NOTE The head shape is more sloped than that of African Dusky Flycatcher, and the overall coloration browner. A summer migrant (October to April). From a distance, size may be deceptive but this species is separated from Pale Flycatcher by the forehead spots.

Length 13 cm
Weight 11 g
Habitat Dense areas of montane and lowland forest.
Habits Usually solitary. Hawks insects from a perch, occasionally flicking its wings while perched.

Call (with comparative track)
A high-pitched, descending *tseeeee* and a distinctive *tsip-ree-ree-ree*, rising in pitch and with a metallic tone.

AT A GLANCE

✔ Plain forehead
✔ Indistinct streaking on underparts
✔ Tiny size

Similar-looking species None

Similar-sounding species Spotted Flycatcher

NOTE The head shape is more rounded than that of Spotted Flycatcher, and the overall coloration is more blue-grey.

STEP TWO – SEPARATING VISUAL GROUPS

Scrub robins

Scrub robins have a typical 'robin' build, but they are browner and more cryptic in appearance than the robin-chats and lack the robin-chats' more vivid coloration. Their tails tend to be more richly coloured, however, and in all species end in white tips. They are often held erect or flicked slowly up and down. The bold facial markings of scrub robins help to identify them as a group, making them unlikely to be confused with any other group, except perhaps chats and wheatears. However, the robin-chats' more secretive behaviour and the combination of tail-flicking and strong facial and wing markings should distinguish them.

Scrub robin calls are melodic and range from repetitive to musical.

The birds forage on the ground, usually within dense vegetation.

> **LOOK FOR**
>
> ✔ wing bars
> ✔ rump coloration
> ✔ tail coloration and markings
> ✔ chest and/or belly coloration and markings
> ✔ presence of a malar stripe
> ✔ bill base and leg colour

SCRUB ROBINS HAVE ONLY ONE VISUAL GROUP

prominent white eyebrow

distinct tail markings

plain brownish coloration

White-browed Scrub Robin

Brown Scrub Robin
Cercotrichas signata
Bruinwipstert

White-browed Scrub Robin
Cercotrichas leucophrys
Gestreepte Wipstert

brown rump

pale underparts

brown wing with striking white alula

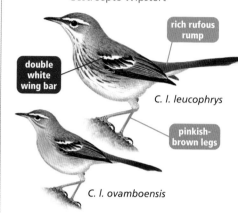

rich rufous rump

double white wing bar

C. l. leucophrys

pinkish-brown legs

C. l. ovamboensis

Length 19 cm **Weight** 35 g
Habitat Moist coastal, mist-belt and riverine forest.
Habits Usually solitary. Shy, moves around in leaf litter on the ground.

Call
A mournful whistle, with some typical robin *chuck* notes and some high-pitched trills.

Length 15 cm **Weight** 20 g
Habitat Varied woodland, including savanna, acacia and miombo.
Habits In pairs. Forages on the ground, usually under cover of vegetation.

Call (with comparative track)
Bubbly and musical, with bulbul- or thrush-like characteristics, as well as typical robin whistles and trills.

AT A GLANCE
✔ Brown rump
✔ Brown wing with striking white alula
✔ Pale underparts
✔ Call

 Similar-looking species None (the combination of brown rump and pale flanks is distinctive)

 Similar-sounding species None

NOTE The dark and white alula should not be confused with the double white wing bar of White-browed Scrub Robin.

AT A GLANCE
✔ Rich rufous rump
✔ Pinkish-brown legs
✔ **Double white wing bar**
✔ **Call**

 Similar-looking species None (the double wing bar is distinctive)

 Similar-sounding species None

NOTE The northeastern race *ovamboensis* lacks streaking on the chest. Take care not to confuse this species' double white wing bar with the dark and white alula of Brown Scrub Robin.

Kalahari Scrub Robin
Cercotrichas paena
Kalahariwipstert

Rufous-tailed Scrub Robin
Cercotrichas galactotes
Rooistertwipstert

wing lacks double white bar

rich rufous rump

black to brownish legs

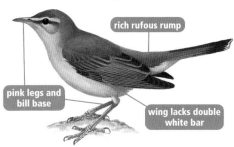

rich rufous rump

pink legs and bill base

wing lacks double white bar

Length 15 cm **Weight** 24 g
Habitat Single record at Zeekoevlei in Cape Town. Usually prefers orchards and similar artificial habitats.
Habits Behaves similarly to other scrub robins in our region, foraging on the ground close to cover.

Length 16 cm **Weight** 20 g
Habitat Drier areas, particularly sandveld, moving on bare ground and in open areas with scrub.
Habits Solitary or in pairs. Forages on the ground.

Call (with comparative track)
A series of varied whistles, chirps and other typical robin sounds, with a similar feel to the complex parts of a Cape Robin-Chat call but lacking the rising whistle at the beginning of each phrase. Also resembles the call of Karoo Thrush but not as full sounding.

Call (with comparative track)
A series of varied whistles, chirps and other typical robin sounds, usually including a distinctive *see-seeooo, see-seeeooo.*

AT A GLANCE

✔ Rich rufous rump
✔ Wing lacks double white bar
✔ Black to brownish legs
✔ Call

Similar-looking species Rufous-tailed Scrub Robin

Similar-sounding species None

NOTE May have brownish legs but never as pink as those of Rufous-tailed Scrub Robin. Any coloration on the lower mandible is minimal.

AT A GLANCE

✔ Rich rufous rump
✔ Wing lacks double white bar
✔ Pink legs and bill base
✔ Call

Similar-looking species Kalahari Scrub Robin

Similar-sounding species None

NOTE Legs noticeably pink compared to some Kalahari Scrub Robins that exhibit brownish legs. Pink on lower mandible is extensive.

Karoo Scrub Robin
Cercotrichas coryphoeus
Slangverklikker

Length 17 cm **Weight** 19 g
Habitat Usually open ground among low Karoo bushes.
Habits Often in pairs. Forages on the ground, running or hopping over the open ground between bushes.

Call
A series of sparrow- and warbler-like notes (the most warbler-like of all scrub robin calls).

AT A GLANCE

✔ Grey-brown rump
✔ Plain brown wing
✔ Dark underparts
✔ Call

 Similar-looking species None (the combination of brown rump and brown flanks is distinctive)

 Similar-sounding species None

Typical habitats for this visual group

Escarpment and mist-belt forests are home to the secretive Brown Scrub Robin.

When looking for Karoo Scrub Robin, the best places to look are the more arid areas of the country.

Acacia woodland is the ideal habitat for White-browed Scrub Robin.

STEP TWO – SEPARATING VISUAL GROUPS
Chats & wheatears

Chats in general are dull brown or pale birds with strongly patterned tails, as are the non-breeding wheatears (Pied, Northern and Isabelline) that occur in southern Africa as vagrants and the juvenile Capped Wheatear. Although similar in some respects to flycatchers, chats have noticeably longer legs and their tail markings and rump colour are distinctive. Separating some members of this group can be tricky, and it helps to concentrate on tail and rump colour and markings. Underwing colour also plays an important role in identifying species and, although this is often difficult to discern, persistence and careful attention to this feature will pay dividends. A series of photographs taken as a bird is flying off can help to determine underwing colour. Unlike flycatchers, chats and wheatears forage on the ground, although they may perch prominently at the top of a low bush or on a post. Some species habitually flick their wings. Although some chat calls are distinctive, many are not and a number of species are best identified visually. Note that the migrant wheatears (Pied, Northern and Isabelline) and the Whinchat are extremely rare vagrants. Some wheatears may superficially resemble pipits, but their legs are black, whereas those of pipits are light pinkish to orange.

LOOK FOR
- ✔ tail coloration/ markings
- ✔ lower back coloration (including number of colours)
- ✔ underpart and underwing coloration
- ✔ relative wing projection
- ✔ facial markings
- ✔ size

CHATS & WHEATEARS CAN BE DIVIDED INTO THREE VISUAL GROUPS

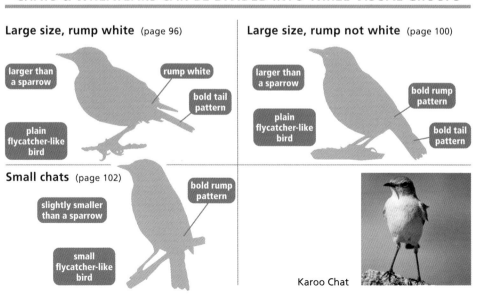

Large size, rump white (page 96)

larger than a sparrow

rump white

bold tail pattern

plain flycatcher-like bird

Large size, rump not white (page 100)

larger than a sparrow

bold rump pattern

plain flycatcher-like bird

bold tail pattern

Small chats (page 102)

slightly smaller than a sparrow

bold rump pattern

small flycatcher-like bird

Karoo Chat

Pied Wheatear
(non-breeding male & female)
Oenanthe pleschanka
Bontskaapwagter

non-breeding ♂

two-tone lower back (light brown and white)

♀

does not flick wings

contrasting mottled throat

comparatively long tail and short wing projection

Length 15 cm; tail 5.3–6.3 cm (female);
wing 8.5–9.8 cm (female) **Weight** 20 g
Habitat Stony arid regions with scattered scrub and trees.
Habits Usually solitary. Perches on trees and bushes, but hawks insects from the ground.

Call
A piercing mix of typical wheatear warbles and mimicry, with a canary-like quality. Best identified visually.

AT A GLANCE

Non-breeding male
- ✔ Does not flick wings
- ✔ Two-tone lower back (light brown and white)
- ✔ Contrasting mottled throat

Female
- ✔ Does not flick wings
- ✔ Two-tone lower back (light brown and white)
- ✔ Comparatively long tail and short wing projection

 Similar-looking species Capped, juvenile (page 97), Northern, female (page 98) and Isabelline (page 98) wheatears

 Similar-sounding species Capped, juvenile (page 97), Northern, female (page 98) and Isabelline (page 98) wheatears; Buff-streaked Chat (page 101)

NOTE Female Northern and Pied wheatears are very difficult to separate, and the relative wing and tail lengths provide the best clue. Pied Wheater is a very rare vagrant.

Female

Capped Wheatear
(juvenile)
Oenanthe pileata
Hoëveldskaapwagter

grey to dark underwing coverts

does not flick wings

three-tone lower back (light brown, buff and white)

Length 17 cm **Weight** 25 g
Habitat Ranges from short grassland to semi-arid areas and cropland. Also found on recently burned land.
Habits Usually solitary or in pairs, sometimes in groups. Often perches on mounds, posts or stones. Forages mainly on the ground. Monogamous breeder.

Call
A piercing mix of typical wheatear warbles and mimicry, with a very scratchy and warbler-like quality. Best identified visually.

AT A GLANCE

✔ Does not flick wings
✔ Three-tone lower back (light brown, buff and white)
✔ Grey to dark underwing coverts

 Similar-looking species Pied, female (page 96), Northern, female and non-breeding male (page 98) and Isabelline (page 98) wheatears

Similar-sounding species Pied (page 96), Northern (page 98) and Isabelline (page 98) wheatears; Buff-streaked Chat (page 101)

Isabelline Wheatear
Oenanthe isabellina
Isabellaskaapwagter

pale white underwing coverts

three-tone lower back (dull brown, rich brown and white)

does not flick wings

Length 16 cm **Weight** 30 g
Habitat Semi-arid areas with low bushes or scattered trees.
Habits Usually solitary. Perches prominently but forages on the ground, often raising its wings as it darts after prey and then revealing its underwing coverts.

Call
A piercing mix of typical wheatear warbles and mimicry, with a canary-like quality. Best identified visually.

AT A GLANCE

✔ Does not flick wings
✔ Three-tone lower back (dull brown, rich brown and white)
✔ Pale white underwing coverts

 Similar-looking species Pied, female (page 96), Capped, juvenile (page 97) and Northern, female wheatears

 Similar-sounding species Pied (page 96), Capped (page 97) and Northern wheaters; Buff-streaked Chat (page 101)

NOTE A very rare vagrant.

Northern Wheatear
(female & non-breeding male)
Oenanthe oenanthe
Europese Skaapwagter

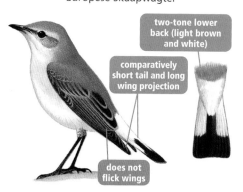

two-tone lower back (light brown and white)

comparatively short tail and long wing projection

does not flick wings

Length 15 cm; tail 4.7–6.3 cm; wing 9.1–10.4 cm **Weight** 25 g
Habitat Dry areas with short grass, degraded woodland and the vicinity of rural settlements.
Habits Usually solitary and may be territorial, even on migration.

Call
A piercing mix of typical wheatear warbles and mimicry, with a canary-like quality; more piercing and less canary-like than that of Pied Wheatear. Best identified visually.

AT A GLANCE

✔ Does not flick wings
✔ Comparatively short tail and long wing projection
✔ Two-tone lower back (light brown and white)

 Similar-looking species Pied, female (page 96,) Capped, juvenile (page 97 and Isabelline wheatears

 Similar-sounding species Pied (page 96) and Isabelline wheatears; Buff-streaked Chat (page 101)

NOTE Female Northern and Pied wheatears are very difficult to separate, and the relative wing and tail lengths provide the best clue. A rare vagrant.

Karoo Chat
(all except *C. s. pollux*)
Cercomela schlegelii namaquensis / bengualensis
Karoospekvreter

two-tone lower back (pale grey and narrow white)

flicks wings infrequently

outer-tail feathers mainly dark but outermost white to tip

Length 17 cm **Weight** 32 g
Habitat Dwarf shrubland in dry areas.
Habits Often perches in the open. Flicks wings infrequently and usually only once.

Call
Five scratchy notes, like counting one-two-three-four-five, with three and four at a slightly higher pitch. Similar to that of Common Myna.

AT A GLANCE

✔ Flicks wings infrequently
✔ Two-tone lower back (pale grey and narrow white)
✔ Outer-tail feathers mainly dark but outermost white to tip
✔ **Call**

Similar-looking species Tractrac Chat

Similar-sounding species None

NOTE Some dark-form Karoo Chats (page 101) have pale grey uppertail coverts and may be inadvertently placed in this group. Nevertheless, heeding the pointers will produce a correct identification. Most of the tail is dark, with only a very narrow, tapering white edge.

Tractrac Chat
Cercomela tractrac
Woestynspekvreter

two-tone lower back (pale grey and extensive white)

flicks wings infrequently

outer-tail feathers mainly white with black tips

Namib form

Length 14 cm **Weight** 20 g
Habitat Arid regions on open plains with grass and small bushes. Also dune shrubland.
Habits Perches in the open and flicks wings (but less than Familiar Chat). Easily disturbed and can be difficult to approach.

Call
An excited jumble of typical chat chirps, notes similar to those of South African Cliff Swallow, and kestrel-like descending notes.

AT A GLANCE

✔ Flicks wings infrequently
✔ Two-tone lower back (pale grey and extensive white)
✔ Outer-tail feathers mainly white with black tips

Similar-looking species Karoo Chat

Similar-sounding species Sclater's Lark (page 73)

NOTE The western race is very pale. Capped, Isabelline, Pied and Northern wheatears also have the inverted 'T' on the tail.

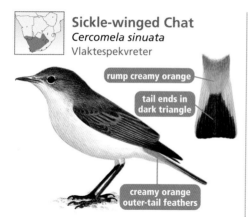

Sickle-winged Chat
Cercomela sinuata
Vlaktespekvreter

rump creamy orange

tail ends in dark triangle

creamy orange outer-tail feathers

Length 15 cm **Weight** 19 g
Habitat Ranges from Karoo scrub to bushy mountain slopes.
Habits Perches in the open. Flies from bush to bush and flicks wings more readily than Karoo Chat, usually twice.

Call
A range of sounds, including *preeu-preeu* (like a budgerigar) and *chik-chik-chik-trrrr* (like Rattling Cisticola).

Familiar Chat
Cercomela familiaris
Gewone Spekvreter

bright rufous rump

bright rufous tail

dark inverted 'T' on tail extends to rump

Length 15 cm
Weight 22 g
Habitat Rocky and hilly areas in open woodland, extending into Karoo. Also gardens.
Habits Habituated to human presence and often found around picnic sites. Flicks wings a number of times after landing.

Call
A distinctive *chirp-chit-chit* sequence. Also a series of warbler-like notes interspersed with a scratchy sound, like grinding teeth.

AT A GLANCE
✔ Bright rufous tail
✔ Bright rufous rump
✔ Dark inverted 'T' on tail extends to rump
✔ Call

 Similar-looking species Sickle-winged Chat

 Similar-sounding species None

NOTE The less pronounced white eye-ring and lack of buff edging to the wing coverts help to separate this species from Sickle-winged Chat.

AT A GLANCE
✔ Creamy orange outer-tail feathers
✔ Rump creamy orange
✔ Tail ends in dark triangle

 Similar-looking species Familiar Chat

 Similar-sounding species Rattling Cisticola (page 50)

NOTE The more pronounced white eye-ring and the buff edging to the wing coverts help to separate this species from Familiar Chat.

Buff-streaked Chat (female)
Oenanthe bifasciata
Bergklipwagter

Karoo Chat (*C. s. pollux*)
Cercomela schlegelii
Karoospekvreter

heavily streaked buff underparts

buff rump

rump uniform grey or two-tone (pale and dark grey)

Length 17 cm **Weight** 33 g
Habitat Rocky parts of montane grassland and near rural settlements.
Habits Solitary, in pairs or in small groups. Shy, but often seen prominently perched some distance away. Hawks insects as well as foraging on the ground.

Call
A rich mix of full-sounding warbles and mimicry.

Length 17 cm
Weight 32 g
Habitat Dwarf shrubland in Karoo, seldom venturing into gardens.
Habits Often perches in the open. Flicks wings infrequently and usually only once.

Call
Five scratchy notes, like counting one-two-three-four-five, with three and four at a slightly higher pitch. Similar to that of Common Myna.

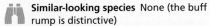

AT A GLANCE

✔ Rump uniform grey or two-tone (pale and dark grey)
✔ Call

Similar-looking species None (the grey rump is distinctive)

Similar-sounding species None

NOTE Some dark-form Karoo Chats have pale grey uppertail coverts that may be mistaken for a white rump, placing the bird in the wrong visual group (see also pale-form Karoo Chat, page 99). Nevertheless, the pointers will produce a correct identification. Most of the tail is dark, with only a very narrow, tapering white edge.

AT A GLANCE

✔ Heavily streaked buff underparts
✔ Buff rump

Similar-looking species None (the buff rump is distinctive)

Similar-sounding species Pied (page 96), Capped (page 97), Isabelline (page 98) and Northern (page 98) wheaters

NOTE Although the male has a white rump, his other markings are distinctive enough to make confusion with other chats unlikely.

African Stonechat (female)
Saxicola torquatus
Gewone Bontrokkie

white rump

Length 14 cm **Weight** 15 g
Habitat Grassy slopes, grassland with bushes, edges of forest and wetland.
Habits Perches in the open and often flicks its tail and wings in typical chat fashion. Very rarely forages on the ground (as Whinchat does), preferring to hawk insects.

Call
A series of canary-like trills and warbles. Contact and alarm call is a distinctive *tseeet-tchik-tchik* or a repeated *tchik-tchik*.

AT A GLANCE

✔ White rump
✔ Call

 Similar-looking species Whinchat, female

 Similar-sounding species None

NOTE Juvenile African Stonechat has a brown rump but the rump lacks the black streaks of Whinchat. The mottled plumage of juveniles and unstreaked rump prevent confusion with Whinchat.

Whinchat
(female & non-breeding male)
Saxicola rubetra
Europese Bontrokkie

brown rump with black streaks

Length 13 cm **Weight** 14 g
Habitat Grassland and wetland with suitable perches, as well as wetland and forest edges.
Habits Forages on the ground, hopping rapidly and occasionally running. Perches in the open.

Call
Usually silent in Africa. Jumbled canary-like phrases, including some mimicry, and *tik-tik* or *hwee-tik-tik*.

AT A GLANCE

✔ Brown rump with black streaks

 Similar-looking species African Stonechat, female

 Similar-sounding species None

NOTE A rare vagrant. Although juvenile African Stonechat also has a brown rump, the mottled plumage and lack of black streaks on the rump will prevent confusion with Whinchat.

STEP TWO – SEPARATING VISUAL GROUPS

Weavers

Weavers are small to medium-sized sparrow-like birds that, being seedeaters, tend to have strong, stout bills and generally hop as they forage on the ground. In the breeding season the males are mostly brightly coloured and can easily be identified. The females and non-breeding males, however, are duller and less conspicuous in tones of soft brown and green to pale yellow. They are most likely to be confused with female and non-breeding male bishops and their allies and also with canaries. Their coloration is subtly greener than the buff tones of the bishop group, and they are noticeably larger than canaries. In general, it helps to become familiar with the overall shape of weavers compared with other similar seedeaters.

These species are mainly sedentary, although some are nomadic in response to the availability of food. All species build extravagant woven nests that are either attached to strong reeds over water or hang from the ends of bare branches.

Many weavers utter a distinctive 'swizzling' call, like a nasal buzzing.

LOOK FOR

- ✔ back colour and/or markings
- ✔ belly and/or chest coloration
- ✔ colour of bill, legs and eyes

WEAVERS CAN BE DIVIDED INTO THREE VISUAL GROUPS

Greenish-yellow mantle, reddish-orange to dark eye (page 104)

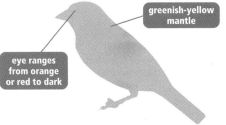

greenish-yellow mantle

eye ranges from orange or red to dark

Southern Masked Weaver

Greyish to brown mantle (page 106)

greyish to brown mantle

Greenish-yellow mantle, pale eye (page 108)

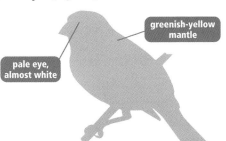

greenish-yellow mantle

pale eye, almost white

Southern Masked Weaver
(female & non-breeding male)
Ploceus velatus
Swartkeelgeelvink

coverts more broadly dark centered

greenish-olive rump

median coverts tipped buff

Length 15 cm **Weight** 33 g
Habitat Open and cultivated areas, woodland, parks and gardens. Associated with water.
Habits Occurs in flocks, gathering at nesting/roosting areas at dusk.

Call (with comparative track)
Typical weaver 'swizzling' but rising and followed by a descending *zeeeeeeoooooo*. Includes raspy chuckles.

AT A GLANCE

✔ Greenish-olive rump
✔ Median coverts tipped buff
✔ Coverts more broadly dark centered

 Similar-looking species Eastern Golden and Southern Brown-throated (page 105) weavers

 Similar-sounding species Eastern Golden, Cape (page 105) and Village (106) weavers

NOTE The uniform olive wash to the back and crown separates this species from Village Weaver, which has a greyish back. Care needs to be taken when separating this species from Eastern Golden Weaver. The patterning and tips of the median coverts separate the species, and familiarity with both is useful.

Eastern Golden Weaver
(female & non-breeding male)
Ploceus subaureus
Geelwewer

coverts narrowly dark centered

greenish-olive rump

median coverts tipped yellow

Length 13 cm **Weight** 30 g
Habitat Breed in reed beds and associated habitats around water but will move into neighbouring savanna in winter.
Habits Usually in flocks and often mixes with other species. Also roosts in reed beds in mixed flocks.

Call
Typical weaver 'swizzling' but lacks the rising and falling 'sigh' of Southern Masked. Includes raspy chuckles.

AT A GLANCE

✔ Greenish-olive rump
✔ Median coverts tipped yellow
✔ Coverts narrowly dark centered

 Similar-looking species Southern Masked and Southern Brown-throated (page 105) weavers

 Similar-sounding species Southern Masked and Village (page 106) weavers

NOTE The uniform olive wash to the back and crown separate this species from Village Weaver, which has a greyish back. Care needs to be taken when separating this species from Southern Masked Weaver. The patterning and tips of the median coverts separate, and familiarity with both these species is useful.

Cape Weaver
(female & non-breeding male)
Ploceus capensis
Kaapse Wewer

long, heavy, pointed bill

Length 18 cm **Weight** 46 g
Habitat Open areas with water and small clumps of trees or bushes.
Habits Occurs in flocks, often associating with other weaver species.

Call (with comparative track)
A series of 'swizzling' notes like a playing card against bicycle spokes speeding up and slowing down.

Southern Brown-throated Weaver
(female & non-breeding male)
Ploceus xanthopterus
Bruinkeelwewer

cinnamon wash to rump

Length 15 cm **Weight** 24 g
Habitat Mainly reed beds, although it moves to forest and woodland to feed.
Habits In pairs or small flocks, foraging in trees and bushes rather than on the ground.

Call
Typical weaver 'swizzling' but includes drawn-out nasal sounds like the soft crying of a baby and some high-pitched canary-like notes.

AT A GLANCE

✔ Long, heavy, pointed bill

 Similar-looking species None (the olive coloration and comparatively long bill are distinctive)

 Similar-sounding species Southern Masked (page 104) and Village (page 106) weavers

AT A GLANCE

✔ Cinnamon wash to rump
✔ Call

 Similar-looking species Southern Masked and Eastern Golden weavers (page 104)

 Similar-sounding species None

Village Weaver
(female & non-breeding male)
Ploceus cucullatus
Bontrugwewer

Red-headed Weaver
(female & non-breeding male)
Anaplectes melanotis
Rooikopwewer

mottled grey back contrasts with olive-green nape

plain grey back contrasts with mustard-yellow nape

Length 16 cm
Weight 34 g
Habitat Wooded and forested areas, including parks and gardens. Usually associated with water.
Habits Usually occurs in flocks, gathering at nesting/roosting areas at dusk.

Call (with comparative track)
Typical weaver 'swizzling' but includes what sounds like high-pitched machine-gun fire.

✔ Mottled grey back contrasts with olive-green nape

Similar-looking species None

Similar-sounding species Southern Masked (page 104) and Cape (page 105) weavers

NOTE The greyish back and greenish crown separate this species from Southern Masked Weaver and other similar weavers, which have uniform greenish upperparts.

Length 14 cm **Weight** 22 g
Habitat Woodland ranging from broad-leaved to acacia and miombo.
Habits Solitary or in pairs. Forages mainly from the ground and will sometimes hawk insects.

Call

A combination of nasal *zeep* and *chirrup* notes like those of Bushveld Pipit and typical weaver 'swizzles' similar to those of Cape Weaver but thinner and at a higher pitch.

AT A GLANCE

✔ Plain grey back contrasts with mustard-yellow nape
✔ Call

Similar-looking species None

Similar-sounding species None

Chestnut Weaver
(female & non-breeding male)
Ploceus rubiginosus
Bruinwewer

crown, nape and mottled back brownish and buff

Typical habitats for this visual group

Length 14 cm **Weight** 30 g
Habitat Thornveld and riverine woodland.
Habits Occurs in flocks, foraging mainly on grasses. Breeds colonially, with several hundred nests in one tree.

Call ▐█▐█▐█▐ █▐▐█▌█▐▐█▐ █ ▐█▌
A series of well-spaced, wader-like *cheeeu* notes.

AT A GLANCE

✔ Crown, nape and mottled back brownish and buff
✔ Call

 Similar-looking species None (the brown rump and generally brown upperparts are distinctive)

Similar-sounding species None

NOTE Beware of confusion with female and non-breeding male bishops and widowbirds. Juveniles have a lightly streaked chest.

Weavers occur in a wide range of habitats, from woodland (top) to forest, cultivated lands (middle) and even gardens (above). Some species, like the Chestnut Weaver, are only found in thornveld and riverine woodland. Others, such as the Red-headed Weaver, prefer broad-leaved, acacia and miombo woodlands.

Lesser Masked Weaver
(female & non-breeding male)
Ploceus intermedius
Kleingeelvink

Holub's Golden Weaver
(female & non-breeding male)
Ploceus xanthops
Goudwewer

blue-grey legs

pinkish-brown legs

Length 14 cm **Weight** 20 g
Habitat Reed beds, woodland and forest.
Habits Occurs mainly in flocks. Forages in trees.

Call
Typical weaver 'swizzling' but as if played at
high speed.

Length 16 cm **Weight** 37 g
Habitat Woodland and savanna, breeding over
water.
Habits Solitary or in pairs. Territorial pairs may
show aggression towards other members of this
family.

Call
A staccato chirp reminiscent of a White-throated
Swallow or Cape Sparrow.

AT A GLANCE

✔ Blue-grey legs
✔ Call

 Similar-looking species None (the
combination of white eyes and blue-
grey legs is distinctive)

 Similar-sounding species None

AT A GLANCE

✔ Pinkish-brown legs
✔ Call

 Similar-looking species None (the
combination of white eyes and pinkish-
brown legs is distinctive)

 Similar-sounding species None

STEP TWO – SEPARATING VISUAL GROUPS

Bishops & allied species

Female and non-breeding male bishops and their allies – whydahs and paradise-whydahs, widowbirds, indigobirds, queleas and the Cuckoo Finch – make up a cryptically coloured group of birds that look very similar in varying shades of brown. They are very difficult to separate, with the exception of some non-breeding males that have coloured patches on the shoulder (the colour, yellow or red, is the same as that in their often flamboyant breeding plumage). Underwing coloration can be important, especially among widowbirds. It is not easy to see, but look out for it when the bird takes off: the Fan-tailed Widowbird, for example, often reveals a flash of cinnamon. Similarly, the length of the tail in non-breeding birds can be significant when placing a bird in a visual group. To help you become familiar with the differences in length, even when they are subtle, we have included the relevant measurements for non-breeding birds where appropriate.

Like other seedeaters, bishops and their allies have strong, conical bills. As a group, they generally have browner and more buff-coloured plumage compared to female and non-breeding weavers, whose coloration is more greenish. When distinguishing between the groups, it helps to become familiar with their overall shape as well as subtle colour differences: members of the bishop family, for instance, appear larger and plumper than canaries.

These species forage on the ground, noticeably hopping as they do so. Unlike weavers, most of them occur almost exclusively in grasslands and wetlands, where they often build their nests in reed beds. The males of this group are mostly polygynous, having several successive mates in the course of a single breeding season. The whydahs, indigobirds and Cuckoo Finch are brood parasites, laying their eggs in other species' nests.

The calls of bishops and allied species are not unlike the 'swizzling' calls of weavers, but in many cases they are even more musical and in some instances more metallic. Indigobird calls play a crucial role in correctly identifying these species in all plumages. They comprise a series of rapid, jumbled sounds that include the mimicked calls of the indigobird's host species. The call excluding the mimicry varies significantly from one region to the next, and it is only the imitation of the host's call (both song and begging) that remains constant within a species. The comparative tracks are helpful in not only indicating what to listen for, but in including excerpts of the hosts' calls.

LOOK FOR

✔ head markings
✔ streaking on the chest
✔ coloration of underwing and underparts
✔ size of bill
✔ overall size of bird
✔ tail length
✔ call, especially mimicked part

Head not broadly striped, tail short, bill or eye-ring diagnostic (page 111)

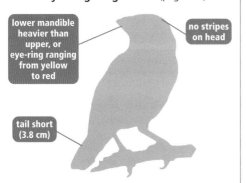

lower mandible heavier than upper, or eye-ring ranging from yellow to red

no stripes on head

tail short (3.8 cm)

Head broadly striped (page 112)

broadly striped head

Head not broadly striped, tail short, bill dull and symmetrical (page 116)

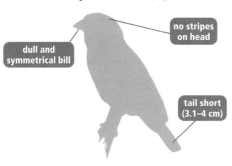

no stripes on head

dull and symmetrical bill

tail short (3.1–4 cm)

Head not broadly striped, tail comparatively long, coloured wing patch (page 119)

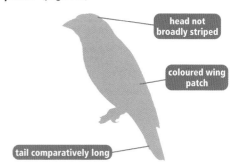

head not broadly striped

coloured wing patch

tail comparatively long

Head not broadly striped, tail comparatively long, no coloured wing patch (page 122)

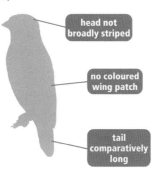

head not broadly striped

no coloured wing patch

tail comparatively long

Yellow-mantled Widowbird (non-breeding male)

Cuckoo Finch
(female & non-breeding male)
Anomalospiza imberbis
Koekoekvink

short, heavy bill with deeper lower mandible

Length 13 cm **Weight** 20 g
Habitat Open woodland and croplands.
Habits Solitary or in pairs. Lays eggs in a wide range of cisticola and prinia nests.

Call
Nondescript chirps. The breeding male emits a soft, garbled mix of parrot-like notes.

AT A GLANCE

✔ Short, heavy bill with deeper lower mandible
✔ Call

 Similar-looking species None (the heavy bill is distinctive)

 Similar-sounding species None

Red-billed Quelea
(female & non-breeding male)
Quelea quelea
Rooibekkwelea

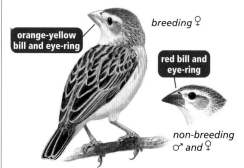

breeding ♀

orange-yellow bill and eye-ring

red bill and eye-ring

non-breeding ♂ and ♀

Length 12 cm
Weight 20 g
Habitat Thornveld, grassland and croplands.
Habits In huge flocks, like moving clouds when in flight. Monogamous.

Call (with comparative track)
Nondescript chirps. The breeding male emits weaver-like 'swizzling' sounds, like Cape Weaver, with additional soft whistles.

AT A GLANCE

Breeding female
✔ Orange-yellow bill and eye-ring
Non-breeding male and female
✔ Red bill and eye-ring

 Similar-looking species None (the eye-ring is distinctive)

 Similar-sounding species Cape Weaver (page 105); Red-headed Quelea (page 118)

NOTE The breeding male shows a large variation in facial patterning. The coloration of the breeding female's bill and eye-ring ranges from yellow to a deep orange.

Pin-tailed Whydah
(female & non-breeding male)
Vidua macroura
Koningrooibekkie

dark pink to red bill

dark legs

shortish tail

Length 12 cm (breeding male has 22-cm tail) **Weight** 15 g
Habitat Open woodland, grassland, forest edges, croplands and gardens.
Habits Usually in small groups, the males obvious in the breeding season. Lays eggs mainly in Common Waxbill nests.

Call (with comparative track)
Nondescript chirping. The breeding male emits a high-pitched chirping that pulsates as he bobs in his display flight. Sounds fuller and more energetic than that of Red-collared Widowbird.

AT A GLANCE	

✔ Dark legs
✔ Dark pink to red bill
✔ Shortish tail

 Similar-looking species None (the pink bill and grey legs are distinctive)

 Similar-sounding species Red-collared Widowbird (page 122)

NOTE The juvenile is plain and resembles sparrows and juvenile mannikins. The bill of the non-breeding male is almost red, whereas that of the female is duller or dark but always shows some pink.

Shaft-tailed Whydah
(female & non-breeding male)
Vidua regia
Pylstertrooibekkie

pale rufous wash to head with browner and less bold head and face markings

stout, pinkish bill

pinkish legs

Length 11 cm (breeding male has 24-cm tail) **Weight** 15 g
Habitat Dry woodland, except broad-leaved.
Habits Solitary or in pairs. Lays eggs mainly in Violet-eared Waxbill nests.

Call
Nondescript chirping. The breeding male emits a series of canary-like phrases but with more 'swizzling' and some piercing whistles. Also an agitated *chik*.

AT A GLANCE	

✔ Pinkish legs
✔ Stout, pinkish bill
✔ Pale rufous wash to head with browner and less bold head and face markings

 Similar-looking species Village Indigobird, female and non-breeding male (page 115)

 Similar-sounding species Sabota Lark (page 72)

NOTE The juvenile is plain and resembles sparrows and juvenile mannikins. Bill size and head coloration are the best clues when separating female/non-breeding male Shaft-tailed Whydahs and Village Indigobirds.

Long-tailed Paradise-Whydah
(female & non-breeding male)
Vidua paradisaea
Gewone Paradysvink

Broad-tailed Paradise-Whydah
(female & non-breeding male)
Vidua obtusa
Breëstertparadysvink

striped head and face with stripe under eye

dark grey bill

dark legs

striped head and face, no stripe under eye

dark grey bill

dark legs

Length 15 cm (breeding male has 29-cm tail)
Weight 20 g
Habitat Dry, open savanna and woodland.
Habits Usually in flocks. The breeding male is obvious when displaying. Lays eggs mainly in Green-winged Pytilia nests.

Call
Nondescript chirping. The breeding male emits a series of very high-pitched whistles, almost like those of a Spotted Flycatcher, coupled with cackling churring and swallow-like notes.

AT A GLANCE
✔ Dark legs
✔ Dark grey bill
✔ Striped head and face with stripe under eye

 Similar-looking species Broad-tailed Paradise-Whydah, female and juvenile

 Similar-sounding species None

NOTE Sub-adults may lack stripe under eye and also have plainer upperparts.

Length 15 cm (breeding male has 20-cm tail) **Weight** 20 g
Habitat Broad-leaved woodland.
Habits Solitary or in pairs or small flocks. The breeding male is obvious when displaying. Lays eggs mainly in Orange-winged Pytilia nests.

Call
Nondescript chirping. The breeding male emits a series of high-pitched sunbird-like whistles mixed with notes similar to those of Terrestrial Brownbul.

AT A GLANCE
✔ Dark legs
✔ Dark grey bill
✔ Striped head and face, no stripe under eye

 Similar-looking species Long-tailed Paradise-Whydah, female and juvenile

 Similar-sounding species None

NOTE Could be confused with sub-adult Long-tailed Paradise-Whydah, which has a distinct cheek mark and plainer upperparts.

Dusky Indigobird
(female & non-breeding male)
Vidua funerea
Gewone Blouvinkie

white bill

dull buff wash to head and chest with striking dark face and head markings

pinkish to pale legs

Length 11 cm **Weight** 15 g
Habitat Woodland, riverine and montane forest, croplands and gardens.
Habits Solitary or in pairs. Lays eggs in African Firefinch nests.

Call (with comparative track)
Some non-breeding birds mimic the popping rattle of the African Firefinch, but are not nearly as vocal as in the breeding season, when the call is a range of chirps that includes mimicry of the African Firefinch.

||||||| ||||||||||| |||

AT A GLANCE

✔ Pinkish to pale legs
✔ White bill
✔ Dull buff wash to head and chest with striking dark face and head markings
✔ Call

 Similar-looking species Purple, Twinspot (page 115) and Village (northern Zimbabwe race) indigobirds, females and non-breeding males (page 115)

 Similar-sounding species Purple, Twinspot (page 115) and Village (page 115) indigobirds

NOTE Female Dusky and Purple indigobirds are considered inseparable in the field, but the non-breeding male Dusky Indigobird has very red legs. It resembles the pale-billed race of Village Indigobird in northern Zimbabwe, but their ranges do not overlap. All indigobirds are best separated on call due to variable leg and bill colour.

Purple Indigobird
(female & non-breeding male)
Vidua purpurascens
Witpootblouvinkie

white bill

dull buff wash to head and chest with striking dark face and head markings

pinkish to pale legs

Length 10 cm **Weight** 13 g
Habitat Dry woodland, riverine forest and croplands.
Habits Solitary or in pairs. Lays eggs in Jameson Firefinch nests.

Call (with comparative track)
Some non-breeding birds mimic the high-pitched bubbling warble of Jameson's Firefinch, but are not nearly as vocal as in the breeding season, when the call is a range of chirps that includes mimicry of Jameson's Firefinch.

||||||||||||||||||| | |||

AT A GLANCE

✔ Pinkish to pale legs
✔ White bill
✔ Dull buff wash to head and chest with striking dark face and head markings
✔ Call

 Similar-looking species Dusky, Twinspot (page 115) and Village (northern Zimbabwe race) indigobirds, females and non-breeding males (page 115)

 Similar-sounding species Dusky, Twinspot (page 115) and Village (page 115) indigobirds

NOTE Female Purple and Dusky indigobirds are considered inseparable in the field, but the non-breeding male Purple Indigobird has dull pink legs. It resembles the pale-billed race of Village Indigobird in northern Zimbabwe, which has more richly coloured legs. All indigobirds are best separated on call due to variable leg and bill colour.

Twinspot Indigobird
(female & non-breeding male)
Vidua codringtoni
Groenblouvinkie

- white bill
- greyish chest contrasts with paler belly
- pinkish to pale legs

Length 10 cm **Weight** 13 g
Habitat Riverine forest and dense bush.
Habits Solitary or in pairs or groups. Lays eggs in Red-throated Twinspot nests.

Call (with comparative track)
Some non-breeding birds mimic the *tseep-tseep-tseep-trrrrrr* of Red-throated Twinspot, but are not nearly as vocal as in the breeding season, when the call is a range of chirps that includes mimicry of the Red-throated Twinspot.

AT A GLANCE

✔ Pinkish to pale legs
✔ White bill
✔ Greyish chest contrasts with paler belly
✔ Call

 Similar-looking species Dusky (page 114), Purple (page 114) and Village (northern Zimbabwe race) indigobirds, females and non-breeding males

 Similar-sounding species Dusky (page 114), Purple (page 114) and Village indigobirds

NOTE The greyish chest is a useful identifying feature. All indigobirds are best separated on call due to variable leg and bill colour.

Village Indigobird
(female & non-breeding male)
Vidua chalybeata
Staalblouvinkie

- comparatively small pink to red bill (white in *V. c. okavangoensis*)
- dull buff wash to head and chest with striking dark face and head markings
- pinkish to pale legs

Length 11 cm **Weight** 12 g
Habitat Acacia woodland near water and mopane woodland.
Habits Solitary or in small groups; larger flocks when breeding. Parasitises Red-billed Firefinch.

Call (with comparative track)
Includes mimics of the swallow-like calls and chirps of Red-billed Firefinch.

AT A GLANCE

✔ Pinkish to pale legs
✔ Comparatively small pink to red bill (white in *V. c. okavangoensis*)
✔ Dull buff wash to head and chest with striking dark face and head markings
✔ Call

 Similar-looking species Shaft-tailed Whydah (page 112); Dusky (northern Zimbabwe race) (page 114), Purple (page 114) and Twinspot indigobirds.

 Similar-sounding species Dusky (page 114), Purple (page 114) and Twinspot indigobirds

NOTE The pale-billed race in northern Zimbabwe resembles Dusky, Purple and Twinspot indigobirds (its range does not overlap with that of Purple Indigobird). Bill size and head coloration are the best clues when separating Shaft-tailed Whydahs and Village Indigobirds. All indigobirds are best separated on call due to variable leg and bill colour.

Southern Red Bishop
(female & non-breeding male)
Euplectes orix
Rooivink

narrow buff eyebrow

primaries not black

short tail

Length 13 cm; tail 3.8 cm
Weight 23 g
Habitat Open grassland, croplands and reed beds close to water.
Habits Occurs in flocks. Very territorial, the male's display flight characterised by very rapid wingbeats, like a bumblebee's.

Call ▐▐▐▐▐▐▐▐▐▐▐▐▐▐▐▐▐
Nondescript chirps. The breeding male emits a 'swizzling' churring, with a distinctive *ti-teeeeeuuuu*.

Black-winged Bishop
(female & non-breeding male)
Euplectes hordeaceus
Vuurkopvink

heavy bill

primaries black

short tail

Length 12 cm; tail 4 cm **Weight** 22 g
Habitat Vegetation and grassland close to water, often in woodland.
Habits Usually occurs in small flocks. Forages mainly on the ground, but displays from a perch.

Call ▐▐▐▐▐▐▐▐▐▐▐▐▐▐▐▐▐
Nondescript chirps. The breeding male emits a series of typical bishop 'swizzles' mixed with *tseep* notes and a distinctive *chi-chi-zweeee*.

Yellow-crowned Bishop
(female & non-breeding male)
Euplectes afer
Goudgeelvink

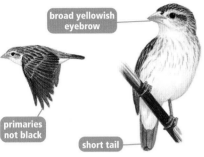

broad yellowish eyebrow

primaries not black

short tail

Length 11 cm; tail 3.7 cm **Weight** 15 g
Habitat Marshy reed beds in breeding season, but moves to drier areas when not breeding.
Habits Usually occurs in flocks.

Call (with comparative track)
Nondescript chirps. The breeding male emits high-pitched *tseeep* notes and a distinctive nasal, insect-like churring. Softer and less metallic than that of Yellow Bishop.

||||||||||||||||||||||||||||||||

AT A GLANCE

 ✔ Short tail
✔ Primaries not black
✔ Broad yellowish eyebrow

 Similar-looking species None (combination of short tail and yellow eyebrow is distinctive)

Similar-sounding species Yellow Bishop (pages 120, 124)

NOTE Slightly longer tails separate the three bishops from the two queleas, which have very short tails.

Typical habitats for this visual group

Almost all of the bishops and their allied species can be found foraging and feeding in a range of grassland habitats.

Reed beds are the favoured breeding habitat for all the bishops.

Due to the abundance of food found in croplands, all the species in this group favour such areas.

Red-headed Quelea
(female & non-breeding male)
Quelea erythrops
Rooikopkwelea

comparatively long bill

bulky appearance

very short tail

Cardinal Quelea
(female & non-breeding male)
Quelea cardinalis
Kardinaalkwelea

very short tail

comparatively short, stubby bill

slender appearance

Length 11 cm; tail 3.3 cm **Weight** 20 g
Habitat Grassland and croplands, usually near water.
Habits In flocks of up to several hundred birds.

Call (with comparative track)
Nondescript chirps. The breeding male emits weaver-like 'swizzling' and twittering with nasal heavy breathing effect; no whistles.

Length 11 cm; tail 3.1 cm **Weight** 13 g
Habitat Tall or lightly wooded grassland.
Habits Occurs in flocks. Nomadic, following rainfall.

Call
Nondescript chirps. The breeding male emits accelerating weaver-like notes, ending in a nasal *meeeuuwww*.

AT A GLANCE

✔ Very short tail
✔ Comparatively long bill
✔ Bulky appearance

 Similar-looking species Cardinal Quelea

 Similar-sounding species Cape Weaver (page 105); Red-billed Quelea (page 111)

NOTE Very difficult to separate from female and non-breeding male Cardinal Quelea, but a significant weight difference makes it appear bulkier and the bill is longer. Also note distribution. Red-headed Quelea is a summer migrant, occurring in the Eastern Cape July–November and in KwaZulu-Natal November–March.

AT A GLANCE

✔ Very short tail
✔ Comparatively short, stubby bill
✔ Slender appearance

 Similar-looking species Red-headed Quelea

 Similar-sounding species None

NOTE Very difficult to separate from female and non-breeding male Red-headed Quelea, but a significant weight difference makes it appear more slender, and it has a short, stubby bill. A rare vagrant.

Fan-tailed Widowbird
(non-breeding male)
Euplectes axillaris
Kortstertflap

red shoulder patch with no white wing bar

Length 16 cm; tail 6.3 cm **Weight** 25 g
Habitat Grassland, reed beds and croplands.
Habits Usually occurs in flocks, associating with other seedeaters.

Call (with comparative track)
Nondescript chirps. The breeding male emits rhythmical, metallic and bubbly notes.

Long-tailed Widowbird
(non-breeding male)
Euplectes progne
Langstertflap

red shoulder patch with white wing bar below

Length 19 cm; tail 9.5 cm **Weight** 40 g
Habitat Grassland and cropland, usually near water.
Habits Usually occurs in flocks.

Call
Nondescript chirps. The breeding male often emits a series of excited *chip-chip-chip-chip* and *churra-churra-churra* notes in display.

AT A GLANCE

 ✔ Red shoulder patch with no white wing bar

Similar-looking species None

Similar-sounding species Yellow-crowned Bishop (page 117)

AT A GLANCE

✔ Red shoulder patch with white wing bar below

 Similar-looking species none

 Similar-sounding species None

Yellow Bishop
(non-breeding male)
Euplectes capensis
Kaapse Flap

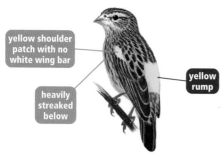

yellow shoulder patch with no white wing bar

yellow rump

heavily streaked below

Length 18 cm; tail 5 cm **Weight** 35 g
Habitat Ranges from coastal fynbos and scrub to high-altitude grassland.
Habits Usually occurs in small family groups.

Call (with comparative track)
Nondescript chirps. The breeding male emits a series of high-pitched *tseep* notes and a more energetic and metallic rattle than that of Yellow-crowned Bishop.

▌▐ ▌ ▌ ▌ ▌▐ ▌▐▐ ▌▐ ▌▐ ▌ ▌▐

AT A GLANCE
✔ Yellow shoulder patch with no white wing bar
✔ Yellow rump
✔ Heavily streaked below

🔭 **Similar-looking species** None (the yellow rump is distinctive)

🦅 **Similar-sounding species** Yellow-crowned Bishop (page 117)

Yellow-mantled Widowbird
(non-breeding male)
Euplectes macroura
Geelrugflap

yellow shoulder patch with no white wing bar

minimal underpart streaking

buff rump

Length 14 cm; tail 6.3 cm **Weight** 21 g
Habitat Wet grassland and reed beds.
Habits Sometimes occurs in flocks when not breeding.

Call ▌▐ ▌ ▌▐ ▌▐ ▌▐▐ ▌ ▌▐▐ ▌▌ ▐▐
Nondescript chirps. The breeding male emits rhythmical *ti-ti-cheeu* notes repeated several times at speed.

AT A GLANCE
✔ Yellow shoulder patch with no white wing bar
✔ Buff rump
✔ Minimal underpart streaking

🔭 **Similar-looking species** None (the bulky tail as well as buff underparts are distinctive)

🦅 **Similar-sounding species** None

White-winged Widowbird
(non-breeding male)
Euplectes albonotatus
Witvlerkflap

yellow shoulder patch with white wing bar

Length 15 cm; tail 5.3 cm **Weight** 20 g
Habitat Grassland and wetland.
Habits Often occurs in flocks when not breeding.

Call (with comparative track)
Nondescript chirps. The breeding male emits a rustling sound, like a small animal in grass, and a metallic rattle very similar to that of River Warbler.

Typical habitats for this visual group

Reed-bed edges are favoured more by White-winged Widowbird than by others in this group.

Moist grassland around pans is ideal for Fan-tailed Widowbird

Long-tailed Widowbird favours typical rank grassland habitats.

AT A GLANCE

✔ Yellow shoulder patch with white wing bar

 Similar-looking species Long-tailed Widowbird (female) (page 123); both have comparatively long tails, but the pale underwing in this species is distinctive

 Similar-sounding species River Warbler (page 26)

White-winged Widowbird (female)
Euplectes albonotatus
Witvlerkflap

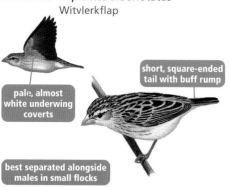

short, square-ended tail with buff rump

pale, almost white underwing coverts

best separated alongside males in small flocks

Length 15 cm; tail 4.5 cm **Weight** 20 g
Habitat Grassland and wetland.
Habits Often occurs in flocks when not breeding.

Call (with comparative track)
Nondescript chirps. The breeding male emits a rustling sound, like a small animal in grass, and a metallic rattle very similar to that of River Warbler.

▌▏▌▐▏▌▐▏▌▐▐▏▌▐▏▌ ▐▌ ▐▌▌

AT A GLANCE

✔ Short, square-ended tail with buff rump
✔ Pale, almost white underwing coverts
✔ Best separated alongside males in small flocks

 Similar-looking species Long-tailed Widowbird (female) (page 123); both have comparatively long tails, but the pale underwing in this species is distinctive

Similar-sounding species River Warbler (page 26)

Note Underwing coverts separate this bird from other female widowbirds, but are difficult to compare in the field. Females are best separated alongside males in the field.

Red-collared Widowbird
(female & non-breeding male)
Euplectes ardens
Rooikeelflap

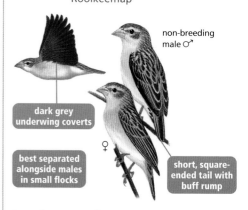

non-breeding male ♂

dark grey underwing coverts

♀

best separated alongside males in small flocks

short, square-ended tail with buff rump

Length 12 cm; tail 4.4 cm (female), 5.5 cm (non-breeding male) **Weight** 20 g
Habitat Grassland, savanna and croplands.
Habits Usually occurs in flocks, associating with other seedeaters when foraging on the ground.

Call (with comparative track)
Nondescript chirps. The breeding male emits high-pitched *chip* notes and a metallic rattle, similar to that of Pin-tailed Whydah but thinner and higher-pitched.

▌▏▌▐▏▌▐▏▌▐▐▏▌▐▏▌▐▌ ▐ ▐▌▌

AT A GLANCE

✔ Short, square-ended tail with buff rump
✔ Dark grey underwing coverts
✔ Best separated alongside males in small flocks

 Similar-looking species Yellow-mantled Widowbird (female) (page 124), but the less bulky tail and smaller bill separate the species.

Similar-sounding species Pin-tailed Whydah (page 112)

Note Underwing coverts separate this bird from other female widowbirds, but are difficult to compare in the field. Females are best separated alongside males in the field.

Fan-tailed Widowbird
(female)
Euplectes axillaris
Kortstertflap

Long-tailed Widowbird
(female)
Euplectes progne
Langstertflap

best separated alongside males in small flocks

cinnamon underwing coverts

short, square-ended tail with buff rump

longer tapering tail

Length 16 cm; tail 4.5 cm **Weight** 25 g
Habitat Grassland, reed beds and croplands.
Habits Usually occurs in flocks, associating with other seedeaters.

Call (with comparative track)
Nondescript chirps. The breeding male emits rhythmical, metallic and bubbly notes.

Length 16 cm; tail 6.2 cm **Weight** 30 g
Habitat Grassland and cropland, usually near water.
Habits Usually occurs in flocks.

Call
Nondescript chirps. The breeding male often emits a series of excited *chip-chip-chip-chip* and *churra-churra-churra* notes in display.

AT A GLANCE

✔ Short, square-ended tail with buff rump
✔ Cinnamon underwing coverts
✔ Best separated alongside males in small flocks

 Similar-looking species None

 Similar-sounding species Yellow-crowned Bishop (page 117)

NOTE Some females are cinnamon-coloured overall. Underwing coverts separate this bird from other female widowbirds, but are difficult to compare in the field. Females are best separated alongside males in the field.

AT A GLANCE

✔ Longer tapering tail

 Similar-looking species White-winged Widowbird (female) (page 122) (both have comparatively long tails)

 Similar-sounding species None

Yellow Bishop
(female)
Euplectes capensis
Kaapse Flap

Yellow-mantled Widowbird (female)
Euplectes macroura
Geelrugflap

shorter tail with yellow rump

best separated alongside males in small flocks

buff underwing coverts

short, square-ended tail with buff rump

Length 14 cm; tail 5.1 cm **Weight** 21 g
Habitat Wet grassland and reed beds.
Habits Sometimes occurs in flocks when not breeding.

Length 15–18 cm; tail 5 cm **Weight** 35 g
Habitat Ranges from coastal fynbos and scrub to high-altitude grassland.
Habits Usually occurs in small family groups.

Call
Nondescript chirps. The breeding male emits rhythmical *ti-ti-cheeu* notes repeated several times at speed.

Call (with comparative track)
Nondescript chirps. The breeding male emits a series of high-pitched *tseep* notes and a more energetic and metallic rattle than that of Yellow-crowned Bishop.

AT A GLANCE
✔ Short, square-ended tail with buff rump
✔ Buff underwing coverts
✔ Best separated alongside males in small flocks

 Similar-looking species None (the bulky tail as well as buff underparts are distinctive)

 Similar-sounding species None

NOTE Underwing coverts separate this bird from other female widowbirds, but are difficult to compare in the field. Females are best separated alongside males in the field.

AT A GLANCE
✔ Shorter tail with yellow rump

 Similar-looking species None (the yellow rump is distinctive)

 Similar-sounding species Yellow-crowned Bishop (page 117)

STEP TWO – SEPARATING VISUAL GROUPS

Sparrows

The common House Sparrow is familiar to everyone and the sight of a small flock foraging on the ground and picking up seeds with its conical, typical seedeater bill enables most people, birders or not, to recognise sparrows as a group (the exception is the Yellow-throated Petronia, which feeds in trees or on rocks and walks rather than hops). Confirmation is provided by the generally grey-brown plumage together with the rich rust coloration on the wings of most species. Bold head markings make the separation of male House, Cape and Great sparrows not too difficult, but identifying the females can be more challenging. The female House Sparrow has dark markings on the back that distinguish it from similarly coloured female bishops, while the broad white eyebrow, pale coloration and small bill of the petronia should help to separate it from similar-looking seedeaters.

LOOK FOR

✔ rump coloration
✔ head markings
✔ wing bars
✔ throat coloration

SPARROWS CAN BE DIVIDED INTO TWO VISUAL GROUPS

Head with markings (page 126)

head markings, notably eyebrow

Head plain grey (page 128)

uniform grey head and face

House Sparrow (male and female)

Great Sparrow

House Sparrow
Passer domesticus
Huismossie

short white eyebrow reaching to bill

grey rump

buff eyebrow

buff back with dark streaks

buff rump

Length 15 cm **Weight** 25 g
Habitat Very common around human settlements.
Habits In pairs or small flocks.

Call (with comparative track)
A typical sparrow *chir-ip* note, but more piercing than that of other sparrows. Also a jumble of *chir-ip* and *zeeu* sounds. The male gives a characteristic *de-zip* territorial call; the female may join in with an agitated chattering. The group contact call is a ratchety rattle.

AT A GLANCE
Male
✔ **Grey rump**
Female
✔ Buff rump
✔ Buff back with dark streaks
✔ Buff eyebrow

Similar-looking species Great Sparrow male resembles the male, but rump colour separates the species; Yellow-throated Petronia (page 127) resembles the female

Similar-sounding species Cape Sparrow (page 127)

Great Sparrow
Passer motitensis
Grootmossie

chestnut side of neck forms 'C' around face

dull chestnut eyebrow

chestnut back with dark streaks

chestnut rump

Length 16 cm **Weight** 32 g
Habitat Acacia woodland. Often found close to water in dry areas.
Habits Solitary or in pairs.

Call (with comparative track)
Slow, drawn-out *chreeuu* notes and agitated chirps.

AT A GLANCE
Male
✔ Chestnut rump
✔ Chestnut back with dark streaks
✔ Chestnut side of neck forms 'C' around face
✔ **Short white eyebrow reaching to bill**
Female
✔ Chestnut rump
✔ Chestnut back with dark streaks
✔ Dull chestnut eyebrow

Similar-looking species House Sparrow male but the rump colour separates the species; Cape Sparrow (female) (page 127) but the chestnut 'C' around the face is distinctive.

Similar-sounding species Lesser and Pallid honeyguides (page 20); Cape (page 127), Southern Grey-headed (page 128) and Northern Grey-headed (page 128) sparrows

Cape Sparrow (female)
Passer melanurus
Gewone Mossie

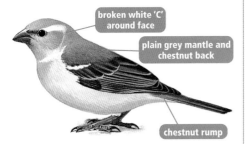

broken white 'C' around face

plain grey mantle and chestnut back

chestnut rump

Length 15 cm **Weight** 29 g
Habitat Varied, from dry areas to woodland, plantations, croplands and human settlements.
Habits Occurs in pairs or flocks, which are sometimes very large. Forages mainly on the ground, but also hawks insects

Call (with comparative track)
At dawn, chirps and similar notes, as *chree-cheeu-chip-cheep*. When in flocks, a series of rattles combined with *cheeu* notes. A group contact call is a short, liquid *churrr-rrr*.

Yellow-throated Petronia
Petronia superciliaris
Geelvlekmossie

broad white eyebrow

bill with horn-coloured upper mandible and pinkish lower mandible

yellow spot on throat (not often visible)

buff back with dark streaks

Length 15 cm
Weight 24 g
Habitat Savanna woodland.
Habits Solitary or in pairs or flocks, moving about restlessly.

Call
Three or four *chirp-chirp-chirp* notes, with distinctive tone and sequence.

AT A GLANCE

✔ Bill with horn-coloured upper mandible and pinkish lower mandible
✔ Buff back with dark streaks
✔ Broad white eyebrow
✔ Yellow spot on throat (not often visible)
✔ Call

Similar-looking species House Sparrow (female) (page 126)

Similar-sounding species African Pipit (page 134)

NOTE The yellow spot on the throat is often hidden. The broad white eyebrow often causes confusion with Streaky-headed Seedeater but the bi-coloured bill and warmer coloured upperparts separate.

AT A GLANCE

✔ Chestnut rump
✔ Plain grey mantle and chestnut back
✔ Broken white 'C' around face

Similar-looking species Great Sparrow (female) (page 126) but the broken white 'C' around the face is distinctive

Similar-sounding species Lesser and Pallid honeyguides (page 20); Great (page 126), Southern Grey-headed (page 128) and Northern Grey-headed (page 128) sparrows

Southern Grey-headed Sparrow
Passer diffusus
Gryskopmossie

obvious white wing bar

compact bill (black in summer and horn-coloured in winter)

greyish throat

Length 15 cm **Weight** 24 g
Habitat Woodland.
Habits Solitary or in pairs. Forages on ground.

Call (with comparative track)
A series of *cheeuu* notes given in sequence and with very little variation. Agitated chirps when competing for food.

AT A GLANCE
✔ Compact bill (black in summer and horn-coloured in winter)
✔ Obvious white wing bar
✔ Greyish throat

Similar-looking species Northern Grey-headed Sparrow

Similar-sounding species Lesser and Pallid honeyguides (page 20); Great (page 126), Cape (page 127) and Northern Grey-headed sparrows

NOTE Head lighter blue-grey and build more slender than in Northern Grey-headed Sparrow. Some Southern Grey-headed Sparrows have paler throats and less distinct wingbar.

Northern Grey-headed Sparrow
Passer griseus
Witkeelmossie

heavy bill (black all year)

white throat

white wing bar inconspicuous or absent

Length 16 cm **Weight** 39 g
Habitat Woodland.
Habits Solitary or in pairs.

Call (with comparative track)
A series of *cheeuu* notes given in sequence and with very little variation. Agitated chirps when competing for food.

AT A GLANCE
✔ Heavy bill (black all year)
✔ White wing bar inconspicuous or absent
✔ White throat

Similar-looking species Southern Grey-headed Sparrow

Similar-sounding species Lesser and Pallid honeyguides (page 20); Great (page 126), Cape (page 127) and Southern Grey-headed sparrows

NOTE Head darker blue-grey and build bulkier than in Southern Grey-headed Sparrow. Some Southern Grey-headed Sparrows have paler throats and less distinct wingbar.

STEP TWO – SEPARATING VISUAL GROUPS

Pipits & longclaws

Being mainly ground-based, pipits are often confused with larks, but there are certain differences between the two groups. Like larks, pipits are small to medium-sized birds, but all species have slender, pointed bills. Pipits are less brightly coloured and less distinctively marked than larks, and they have longer, more slender legs that give them a characteristic gait. The fast pace at which they walk and dart about chasing insects is in stark contrast to larks' slower and more methodical search for seeds. Most pipits can be observed 'tail-wagging', which also helps to separate them from larks.

Pipits are nomadic, so distribution is a less important criterion for identification, especially in winter, when they tend to move around more; in summer, their whereabouts are generally more predictable. Calls can be helpful when separating some species, but for the most part pipits can be identified without paying much attention to their vocalisations. However – and especially if you are just beginning to familiarise yourself with the different pipits – it is useful to identify a bird first on its display call and then to observe how it behaves so that the next time you see it, you will recognise the species from its behaviour.

More important than vocalisations is pipits' habit of tail-wagging, although care should be exercised when the individuals are juvenile. Tail-wagging develops as the birds age, so the action of a youngster can be quite different from that of an adult bird of the same species. In general, juveniles are difficult to separate unless they are seen with adults. Also bear in mind that behavioural characteristics such as tail-wagging are best viewed once the birds have settled and are no longer stressed by your presence. If you are uncertain about an identification, watch the mystery bird for 10–15 minutes and you will get a better idea of its 'normal' behaviour.

Longclaws are closely related to pipits and have a similar build, but adults are easily distinguished by their richly coloured throats with contrasting black markings. Immature birds, however, are more drab in appearance and can be confused with adult pipits.

> **LOOK FOR**
>
> ✔ tail-wagging and other behaviour
> ✔ back and chest markings
> ✔ rump markings
> ✔ tail length and/or length of wing in relation to tail

Long-billed Pipit

Back and flanks streaked (page 131)

streaked back

streaked flanks

Back streaked, flanks not streaked (page 134)

streaked back

flanks not streaked

Back plain (page 136)

plain back

Back scalloped (page 138)

scalloped back

Plain-backed Pipit

Short-tailed Pipit

Anthus brachyurus
Kortstertkoester

mottled dark back

bold streaking on chest

smaller than a sparrow

Length 12 cm **Weight** 16 g
Habitat Short grassland in hilly areas.
Habits Usually solitary or in pairs. Very rarely uses elevated perches.

Call ▌▌▌▌▌▌▌▌▌▌▌▌▌▌
Soft, liquid nasal notes, similar to that of Rudd's Lark.

AT A GLANCE

✔ Smaller than a sparrow
✔ Mottled dark back
✔ Bold streaking on chest

Similar-looking species Bushveld Pipit

Similar-sounding species Rudd's Lark (page 64)

NOTE Can be confused with a non-breeding bishop. A 'bishop' with white outer-tail feathers should be examined more closely.

Bushveld Pipit

Anthus caffer
Bosveldkoester

light-coloured back

smaller than a sparrow

streaking on chest less prominent

Length 13 cm
Weight 17 g
Habitat Open broad-leaved and savanna woodland, and burned areas.
Habits Solitary or in pairs. Usually remains on the ground.

Call ▌▌▌▌▌▌▌▌▌▌▌▌▌▌
A nasal *zeee-ip*, *zeee-oo* that continues rhythmically, and a series of descending nasal notes similar to that of Lesser Striped Swallow but more piercing and without a distinctive rhythm. Also a piercing *dzeep* alarm or flight call.

AT A GLANCE

✔ Smaller than a sparrow
✔ Light-coloured back
✔ Streaking on chest less prominent

 Similar-looking species Short-tailed Pipit

 Similar-sounding species None

NOTE The streaking on the flanks can be minimal and may be obscured by the folded wing, sometimes making the flanks appear plain. Careful observation should be made with any heavily streaked pipit with plain flanks.

Striped Pipit
Anthus lineiventris
Gestreepte Koester

same size as a sparrow

yellow edges to wing feathers

belly and flanks streaked

Length 18 cm **Weight** 34 g
Habitat Rocky areas with broad-leaved woodland.
Habits Usually seen singing from a prominent perch in a tree. Forages among rocks.

Call
Bold and very musical chirps, similar to those of African Pied Wagtail, although phrasing is very variable. Call less thrush-like than that of Tree Pipit.

AT A GLANCE
✔ Same size as a sparrow
✔ Belly and flanks streaked
✔ Yellow edges to wing feathers
✔ Call

 Similar-looking species None (the streaking on the belly and flanks is distinctive)

 Similar-sounding species None

Tree Pipit
Anthus trivialis
Boomkoester

rump not streaked

same size as a sparrow

belly not streaked

Length 14 cm **Weight** 22 g
Habitat Open grassland with large trees.
Habits Solitary or in pairs or small flocks. Flies up into a tree when disturbed.

Call
Only flight and contact calls are heard in southern Africa. Elsewhere, melodic with canary-like phrases, like those of Karoo Thrush. Call not as wagtail-like as that of Striped Pipit.

AT A GLANCE
✔ Same size as a sparrow
✔ Belly not streaked
✔ Rump not streaked
✔ Call

 Similar-looking species Red-throated Pipit (page 133)

 Similar-sounding species None

NOTE A summer migrant (October to April).

Red-throated Pipit
(non-breeding)
Anthus cervinus
Rooikeelkoester

streaked rump

belly not streaked

same size as a sparrow

Length 14 cm **Weight** 20 g
Habitat Short grassland near water.
Habits Probably solitary in the region.

Call

Probably silent in southern Africa. Elsewhere, a very musical, canary-like song comprising various warbles, and a single piercing *dzee* note similar to the single-note call of Cape White-eye, but shorter and harsher.

AT A GLANCE

✔ Same size as a sparrow
✔ Belly not streaked
✔ Streaked rump
✔ Call

 Similar-looking species Tree Pipit (page 132)

 Similar-sounding species None

NOTE A rare vagrant.

Typical habitats for this visual group

Short grassland, often near water, is an ideal habitat for both the Short-tailed and the rare Red-throated Pipit.

The Bushveld Pipit is found in grassland with large trees. Although this habitat is shared by the Tree Pipit, the latter is a less common summer visitor and, due to its hilltopping behaviour, favours clumps of woodland at the tops of hilly areas.

African Pipit
Anthus cinnamomeus
Gewone Koester

distinct and obvious back streaking, never looks plain

A. c. bocagii

A. c. spurium

Length 16 cm; tail 6.2 cm **Weight** 27 g
Habitat Grassland and savanna, usually near water, preferring short grass and burned areas; below 2 000 m.
Habits Solitary or in pairs when breeding; often in groups when not breeding. Runs in bursts, occasionally pumping its tail downward once or twice at the end of a run; sometimes struts 'proudly'.

Call (with comparative track)
In display, a sequence of *chit-chit* notes starting with two and adding another at the end of each phrase, with a long flourish at the end.

AT A GLANCE

✔ Distinct and obvious back streaking, never looks plain
✔ Call
✔ Habitat (altitude)

Similar-looking species Mountain Pipit

Similar-sounding species Mountain Pipit

NOTE African and Mountain pipits may overlap at lower altitudes, where call is an important aid in separating them. As little is known about Mountain Pipit behaviour, the tail wagging of African Pipit may not be truly reliable. Habitat and behaviour separate this species from Wood Pipit. Stronger back and chest markings separate from Long-billed Pipit, which also frequents different habitat.

Mountain Pipit
Anthus hoeschi
Bergkoester

distinct and obvious back streaking, never looks plain

Length 18 cm; tail 6.6 cm **Weight** 27 g
Habitat Montane grassland above 2 000 m, almost entirely restricted to Lesotho.
Habits Solitary or in pairs or small groups. Usually on the ground, but sometimes seen on elevated perches.

Call (with comparative track)
In aerial display, a series of widely spaced, single *chirit* notes with a flurry at the end. Similar to that of African Pipit, but a series of widely spaced notes rather than an increasing sequence.

AT A GLANCE

✔ Distinct and obvious back streaking, never looks plain
✔ Call
✔ Habitat (altitude)

 Similar-looking species African Pipit

 Similar-sounding species African Pipit

NOTE African and Mountain pipits may overlap at lower altitudes, where call is an important aid in separating them. As little is known about Mountain Pipit behaviour, tail wagging as a typical pipit feature has not been adequately described. Habitat and behaviour separate this species from Wood Pipit. Stronger back and chest markings separate from Long-billed Pipit, which also frequents different habitat.

Wood Pipit
Anthus nyassae
Boskoester

Long-billed Pipit
Anthus similis
Nicholsonse Koester

indistinct back streaking, can look plain from a distance

indistinct back streaking, can look plain from a distance

Length 18 cm
Weight 24 g
Habitat Short grass in woodland.
Habits Solitary or in pairs. Usually on the ground, but flies to a perch in a tree when disturbed, sometimes running along a branch.

Length 18 cm **Weight** 30 g
Habitat Rock-strewn slopes in dry and grassy areas; also woodland.
Habits Mostly solitary or in pairs, but occasionally also in small flocks. Usually on the ground, but sometimes uses an elevated perch. Flicks tail weakly and infrequently.

Call (with comparative track)
In display, a repeated five-note sequence:
deeweet-cheoa-prrrree-tzoeu-prrrreuu.

Call (with comparative track)
A series of single-noted, sparrow-like chirps, descending in pitch.

AT A GLANCE

✔ Indistinct back streaking, can look plain from a distance
✔ Habitat
✔ Flies to trees and walks along branches

 Similar-looking species Long-billed Pipit

Similar-sounding species Long-billed, Plain-backed (page 136) and Buffy (page 136) pipits

NOTE The indistinctly streaked back makes this species a candidate for either the streaked back or the plain back group. Like Long-billed Pipit, it will often flush into a tree, but different behaviour and habitat separate the species. Indistinct back markings separate it from African and Mountain pipits.

AT A GLANCE

✔ Indistinct back streaking, can look plain from a distance
✔ Habitat
✔ Sometimes perches on top of bushes and trees but mainly ground based

 Similar-looking species Wood Pipit

 Similar-sounding species Wood, Plain-backed and Buffy (page 136) pipits

NOTE The indistinctly streaked back makes this species a candidate for either the streaked back or the plain back group. Like Wood Pipit, it may flush to the top of an elevated perch, but different behaviour and habitat help separate the species. Indistinct back markings separate from African and Mountain pipits.

Plain-backed Pipit
Anthus leucophrys
Donkerkoester

slender build with less upright stance

two-tone bill with extensive base colour

tail does not wag above rest position

Length 17 cm; tail 6.5 cm **Weight** 27 g
Habitat Sandy and burned areas in very short grassland.
Habits Usually solitary or in pairs, but sometimes in small flocks. Walks upright, but its stance is less upright than that of Buffy Pipit. Tail wagging takes the form of repeated strong downward pumping, the tail not rising above the resting position.

Call (with comparative track)
Mostly a three-noted *zeea-treeu-preeu*, the second note lower than the first and the last note slightly higher than the second; less frequently, a two-noted *zee-zeeoot*.

IIIIIIIIIIIIIIIIIIIIIII

AT A GLANCE

✔ Tail does not wag above rest position
✔ Two-tone bill with extensive base colour
✔ Slender build with less upright stance

Similar-looking species Buffy Pipit

Similar-sounding species Wood (page 135), Long-billed (page 135) and Buffy pipits

NOTE Although upright, the stance of Plain-backed Pipit is not as bolt upright as that of Buffy Pipit, and the chest is less rounded. There is some documented evidence of bill base colour variations, so look for an extensively coloured bill base rather than at the colour. Bill base colour separates this species from African Rock Pipit.

Buffy Pipit
Anthus vaalensis
Vaalkoester

slender build with very upright stance

two-tone bill with extensive base colour

tail wags above and below rest position

Length 18 cm; tail 7.3 cm **Weight** 29 g
Habitat Sandy and burned areas in short grassland.
Habits Usually solitary or in pairs, but sometimes in small flocks. Takes a short run, stops and stands very upright. Raises head from time to time while foraging. Wags tail slowly and deliberately, raising it above and below the resting position.

Call (with comparative track)
A very fast *pree-ree-oo* and a jumble of sparrow-like *treeuu*, *chree* and *preeu* notes with no definite pattern. The alarm call is more like that of a wagtail than of a sparrow.

IIIIIIIIIIIIIIIIIIIIIII

AT A GLANCE

✔ Tail wags above and below rest position
✔ Two-tone bill with extensive base colour
✔ Slender build with very upright stance

Similar-looking species Plain-backed Pipit

Similar-sounding species Long-billed (page 135), Wood (page 135) and Plain-backed pipits

NOTE The stance is more upright and the chest rounder than that of Plain-backed Pipit. There is some documented evidence of bill base colour variations, so look for an extensively coloured bill base rather than at the colour. Bill base colour separates this species from African Rock Pipit.

African Rock Pipit
Anthus crenatus
Klipkoester

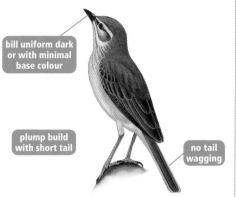

bill uniform dark or with minimal base colour

plump build with short tail

no tail wagging

Length 18 cm; tail 6.2 cm **Weight** 30 g
Habitat Rocky outcrops above 1 000 m.
Habits Either solitary or in pairs. Usually seen as it forages on the ground.

Call
A descending shrill whistle followed by a single- or double-noted trill, like a sound effect in an electronic game.

AT A GLANCE

✔ No tail wagging
✔ Bill uniform dark or with minimal base colour
✔ Plump build with short tail

 Similar-looking species None (the uniform dark bill is distinctive)

 Similar-sounding species None

Note Any bill base colour, if present, is way less extensive than in other species in the group, and is restricted to base third of the bill.

Typical habitats for this visual group

Montane grassland with rocks is the ideal habitat for African Rock Pipit.

Patchy grassland along sand roads will often turn up Buffy Pipit.

Plain-backed Pipit favours short grassland with patches of soil.

Yellow-breasted Pipit
(female & non-breeding male)
Anthus chloris
Geelborskoester

throat and chest the same colour

indistinctly streaked breast band

feathered tibia

Length 17 cm; tail 6.6 cm **Weight** 25 g
Habitat Montane grassland, usually on flatter slopes.
Habits Solitary or in pairs, but sometimes also in small flocks. Stays low and will run rather than fly away when disturbed.

Call
An excited rattle, similar to the sound of a playing card hitting the spokes of a bicycle wheel. Also *cheeu* (like that of a Scarlet-chested Sunbird) or sometimes *too-ee* (like that of a Willow Warbler).

AT A GLANCE

✔ Indistinctly streaked breast band
✔ Feathered tibia
✔ Colour of throat and chest the same
✔ Call

Similar-looking species None

Similar-sounding species None

Golden Pipit (female)
Tmetothylacus tenellus
Goudkoester

no streaking on chest

unfeathered tibia

Length 15 cm; tail 6 cm **Weight** 20 g
Habitat Dry grassland.
Habits Solitary in the region. Perches in trees or on bushes.

Call
A distinctive rhythmical series of sunbird-like chirps, *chit-chit-chiree-chiroo-chit*, sometimes with additional notes at the end. The call is very soft and birds are more likely to be seen before they are heard.

AT A GLANCE

✔ No streaking on chest
✔ Unfeathered tibia
✔ Call

Similar-looking species None (the lack of feathers on the tibia is distinctive)

Similar-sounding species None

NOTE A rare vagrant, mostly November to February.

Cape Longclaw (juvenile)
Macronyx capensis
Oranjekeelkalkoentjie

Typical habitats for this visual group

dull yellow throat contrasts with chest colour

indistinct streaked necklace

feathered tibia

Cape Longclaw is common in most grassland habitats and is often seen on the sides of dust roads.

Length 20 cm; tail 6.6 cm **Weight** 46 g
Habitat Mostly open grasslands ranging from wet to high-altitude.
Habits Usually in pairs. Uses low perches. Often gives a cat-like meow when in flight.

Call
An unmistakable cat-like *meeeuuuwww*. Adult males emit an excited sparrow-like chirping when defending a territory. Birds also produce mournful single whistles about a second apart.

Montane grassland in areas such as Wakkerstroom are good areas to look for Yellow-breasted Pipit.

AT A GLANCE

✔ Indistinct streaked necklace
✔ Feathered tibia
✔ Dull yellow throat contrasts with chest colour
✔ Call

 Similar-looking species None (the indistinct necklace is distinctive)

 Similar-sounding species None

STEP TWO – SEPARATING VISUAL GROUPS

Canaries & allied species

Canaries, seedeaters and siskins make up a large group of seed-eating birds that are recognised by their stout, conical bills. They are generally smaller than sparrows and weavers, and whereas the males are often quite brightly coloured, the females tend to be brown or grey. Apart from the size difference, female canaries and their allies can be distinguished from sparrows in that they lack the latter's combination of warm brown coloration and distinctive plumage patterns.

Also unlike sparrows, which pick up seeds only on the ground, canaries forage on grasses and shrubs too. Their calls are very melodic, comprising bubbly, liquid and tuneful notes.

LOOK FOR

✔ rump coloration
✔ head, face, throat and chest markings
✔ the extent of yellow in the plumage
✔ tips to wings and/or tail

Black-throated Canary (female)

Black-throated Canary (male)

Grey or pale brown overall, with a yellow rump (page 142)

grey or pale brown overall, sometimes with yellow tones

yellow rump

Grey overall, with a grey or brown rump (page 144)

greyish coloration

grey or brown rump

Chestnut or cinnamon overall (page 146)

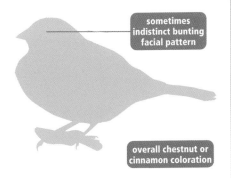

sometimes indistinct bunting facial pattern

overall chestnut or cinnamon coloration

Drab yellow, with plain upperparts (page 147)

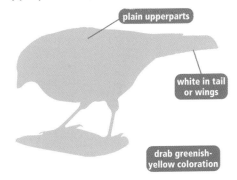

plain upperparts

white in tail or wings

drab greenish-yellow coloration

Black-throated Canary
Crithagra atrogularis
Bergkanarie

small black throat patch

uniform yellow rump

♀

♂

grey-brown throat

pale tips to tail

yellow rump and white uppertail coverts

pale tips to tail

Length 11 cm **Weight** 13 g
Habitat Woodland, grassland and croplands.
Habits In pairs or flocks. Forages on the ground or in trees.

Call (with comparative track)
An energetic series of typical canary notes, with distinctive Cape Sparrow notes and piercing whistles in the phrasing.

AT A GLANCE

Male
✔ Pale tips to tail
✔ Uniform yellow rump
✔ Small black throat patch
Female
✔ Pale tips to tail
✔ Yellow rump and white uppertail coverts
✔ Grey-brown throat

 Similar-looking species Lemon-breasted Canary

Similar-sounding species White-throated Canary (page 143)

NOTE The pale tail tips and white uppertail coverts may be difficult to see if the plumage is worn. Distribution does not overlap with that of Lemon-breasted Canary.

Lemon-breasted Canary
(female)
Crithagra citrinipectus
Geelborskanarie

rump and uppertail coverts uniform yellow

pale tips to tail

pale buffy throat with malar stripe

Length 12 cm **Weight** 11 g
Habitat Woodland, grassland and savanna.
Habits In pairs or flocks. Forages on the ground or in trees.

Call (with comparative track)
Short bursts of jumbled, typical canary or warbler-like phrases, with a pause between each phrase.

AT A GLANCE

✔ Pale tips to tail
✔ Rump and uppertail coverts uniform yellow
✔ Pale buffy throat with malar stripe

 Similar-looking species Black-throated Canary

Similar-sounding species None

NOTE The pale tail tips and white uppertail coverts may be difficult to see if the plumage is worn. Distribution does not overlap with that of Black-throated Canary.

Yellow Canary (female)
Crithagra flaviventris
Geelkanarie

rump and uppertail coverts greenish-yellow

underparts variably streaked

plain brownish and yellow tail lacks white tips

Length 14 cm **Weight** 18 g
Habitat Open shrubland at a range of altitudes.
Habits Usually in flocks, often with other canaries. Forages on the ground.

Call (with comparative track)
A series of typical canary notes without pause; a single phrase can last for up to 20 seconds.

AT A GLANCE
✔ Plain brownish and yellow tail lacks white tips
✔ Rump and uppertail coverts greenish-yellow
✔ Underparts variably streaked

Similar-looking species None (the streaking on the underparts is distinctive)

Similar-sounding species None

NOTE Although usually conspicuous, the streaking on the underparts ranges from heavy to quite pale. Note that a juvenile Cape Canary can resemble a female Yellow Canary with streaky underparts.

White-throated Canary
Crithagra albogularis
Witkeelkanarie

rump and uppertail coverts uniform greenish-yellow

plain underparts lack streaks

plain dark tail lacks white tips

Length 15 cm **Weight** 27 g
Habitat Shrubland, sometimes on rocky slopes.
Habits Usually in pairs or small flocks. Forages on the ground.

Call (with comparative track)
A series of short, typical canary notes with long pauses between phrases. The song is full and liquid, often ending in a Bokmakierie-like *puurr*.

AT A GLANCE
✔ Plain dark tail lacks white tips
✔ rump and uppertail coverts uniform greenish-yellow
✔ Plain underparts lack streaks

Similar-looking species None

Similar-sounding species Black-throated Canary (page 142)

NOTE The bill is one of the heaviest of all seed-eating birds.

Black-eared Seedeater
Crithagra mennelli
Swartoorkanarie

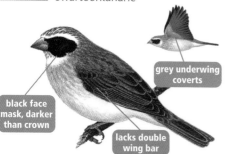

grey underwing coverts

black face mask, darker than crown

lacks double wing bar

Length 13 cm
Weight 15 g
Habitat Woodland associated with Kalahari sand.
Habits Solitary or in pairs or small flocks. Forages on the ground and among bushes.

Call (with comparative track)
Similar basic notes to those of Streaky-headed Seedeater but with jumbled phrases like those of Cape White-eye.

AT A GLANCE

✔ Lacks double wing bar
✔ Black face mask, darker than crown
✔ Grey underwing coverts
✔ Call

 Similar-looking species Dark-cheeked race of Streaky-headed Seedeater

 Similar-sounding species None

NOTE Streaking on the chest of this species and Streaky-headed Seedeater is variable and not a reliable feature; the colour of the underwing coverts is most reliable for separating these species.

Streaky-headed Seedeater
Crithagra gularis
Streepkopkanarie

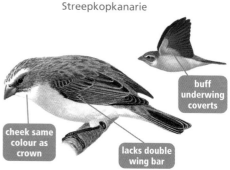

buff underwing coverts

cheek same colour as crown

lacks double wing bar

Length 15 cm **Weight** 20 g
Habitat Various woodland types, in rocky hills and open areas; also forest edges.
Habits Usually in pairs or small flocks. Forages on the ground and in trees; easily missed.

Call (with comparative track)
A wide range of musical notes, including a distinctive, almost parrot-like *si-ree* or *si-ree-oo*.

AT A GLANCE

✔ Lacks double wing bar
✔ Cheek same colour as crown
✔ Buff underwing coverts
✔ Call

 Similar-looking species The dark-cheeked race resembles Black-eared Seedeater

 Similar-sounding species None

NOTE Streaking on the chest of this species and Black-eared Seedeater is variable and not a reliable feature; the colour of the underwing coverts is most reliable for separating these species. *Humilis* race is darker overall but cheeks always match crown.

Protea Seedeater
Crithagra leucoptera
Witvlerkkanarie

double white wing bar

Length 15 cm **Weight** 22 g
Habitat Fynbos, especially protea stands; also dense bush and forest edges.
Habits Solitary or in pairs or small groups. Forages in the canopy of trees and bushes, where it is easily missed.

Call (with comparative track)
A typical canary introductory phrase followed by an agitated series of repeated *chur-chur-chur... tirup-tirup-tirup* notes.

Typical habitats for this visual group

Fynbos and protea stands are home to the range-bound Protea Seedeater.

Forest edges also provide suitable habitat for Protea and Streaky-headed seedeaters.

AT A GLANCE

✔ Double white wing bar
✔ Call

 Similar-looking species None (the double wing bar is distinctive)

 Similar-sounding species None

Black-headed Canary
(female)
Serinus alario
Swartkopkanarie

plain uniform grey head

chestnut wing

chestnut tail

Length 13 cm **Weight** 12 g
Habitat Arid and semi-arid shrubland.
Habits In pairs or small flocks in breeding season; large flocks when not breeding. Forages in bushes and on the ground.

Call (with comparative track)
The most warbler-like of all canary calls, but with weaver-like 'swizzling' and rising nasal whistles.

Lark-like Bunting
Emberiza impetuani
Vaalstreepkoppie

rufous edge to wing feathers

indistinct buff malar stripe and eyebrow on brownish head

brownish tail

Length 14 cm **Weight** 15 g
Habitat Very short grassland, shrublands and rocky outcrops in dry areas.
Habits Usually in small groups, but sometimes in large flocks. Associates with sparrow-larks. Forages on the ground.

Call (with comparative track)
Thrush-like, with a weaver's 'swizzle', often repeated.

Cape Siskin
Crithagra totta
Kaapse Pietjiekanarie

white tips to primaries

white band to entire tip of tail

♀

♂

Length 12 cm **Weight** 11 g
Habitat Montane forest patches and fynbos; also edges of plantations.
Habits Usually in pairs or small flocks, but larger groups also occur. Forages on the ground or on vegetation.

Call (with comparative track)
Almost warbler-like, comprising a series of rising and falling whistles and swizzles.

AT A GLANCE

✔ White band to entire tip of tail
✔ White tips to primaries
✔ Distribution
✔ Call

Similar-looking species None (the white-tipped primaries are distinctive)

Similar-sounding species None

NOTE The white tips to the primaries are not always visible on the female, but the different distributions of Cape and Drakensberg siskins make identification easy.

Drakensberg Siskin
Crithagra symonsi
Bergpietjiekanarie

white in outer-tail feathers with almost no white tipping on tail

♀

♂

primaries lack white tips

Length 13 cm **Weight** 11 g
Habitat Montane grassland and shrublands.
Habits In pairs or flocks. Forages among rocks and grass tufts.

Call (with comparative track)
Very musical and almost identical to a caged canary, with distinctive canary whistles.

AT A GLANCE

✔ White in outer-tail feathers with almost no white tipping on tail
✔ Primaries lack white tips
✔ Distribution
✔ Call

Similar-looking species None (the white outer-tail feathers are distinctive)

Similar-sounding species None

NOTE The white outer-tail feathers are not always visible, but the different distributions of Drakensberg and Cape siskins make identification easy.

APPENDIX

In order that similar-looking species could be grouped together for comparative purposes, strict taxonomic sequences have not been adhered to in the 'family' groups described in this book. For those interested in taxonomic relationships, the groupings in this book are represented by the following families and genera. Note that, taxonomically, warblers comprise a large group that includes cisticolas and prinias (Cisticolidae) as well as 'true' warblers (Sylviidae).

HONEYGUIDES & HONEYBIRDS
Family: Indicatoridae
Genera: *Indicator* (Greater, Lesser, Pallid and Scaly-throated honeyguides); *Prodotiscus* (Brown-backed and Green-backed honeybirds).

TRUE WARBLERS & ALLIED SPECIES
Family: Sylviidae
Genera: *Acrocephalus* (Sedge and Marsh warblers, Greater and Lesser swamp-warblers, and Basra, African, Eurasian and Great reed-warblers); *Sylvia* (Common Whitethroat, Garden Warbler); *Luscinia* (Thrush Nightingale); *Locustella* (River Warbler); *Schoenicola* (Broad-tailed Warbler); *Hippolais* (Olive-tree, Icterine and Upcher's warblers); *Bradypterus* (Barratt's and Knysna warblers, and Little Rush-Warbler); *Phylloscopus* (Willow Warbler).

CISTICOLAS
Family: Cisticolidae
Genera: *Cisticola* (Zitting, Desert, Cloud, Wing-snapping, Pale-crowned, Croaking, Short-winged, Singing, Lazy, Red-faced, Chirping, Rufous-winged, Luapula, Levaillant's, Grey-backed, Tinkling, Wailing and Rattling cisticolas, and Neddicky); *Heliolais* (Red-winged Warbler).

PRINIAS & PRINIA-LIKE WARBLERS
Family: Cisticolidae
Genera: *Prinia* (Tawny-flanked, Black-chested, Drakensberg and Karoo prinias); *Oreophilais* (Roberts's Warbler); *Phragmacia* (Namaqua Warbler).

LARKS & SPARROW-LARKS
Family: Alaudidae
Genera: *Eremopterix* (Black-eared, Chestnut-backed and Grey-backed sparrow-larks); *Heteromirafra* (Rudd's Lark); *Spizocorys* (Botha's, Stark's, Pink-billed and Sclater's larks); *Ammomanopsis* (Gray's Lark); *Certhilauda* (Cape, Agulhas, Karoo, Benguela and Eastern long-billed larks, and Short-clawed Lark); *Chersomanes* (Spike-heeled Lark); *Mirafra* (Eastern and Cape clapper larks, and Monotonous, Flappet, Melodious and Rufous-naped larks); *Calendulauda* (Fawn-coloured, Karoo, Barlow's, Red, Dune and Sabota larks); *Calandrella* (Red-capped Lark); *Pinarocorys* (Dusky Lark); *Galerida* (Large-billed Lark).

FLYCATCHERS
Family: Muscicapidae
Genera: *Bradornis* (Marico, Pale and Chat flycatchers); *Muscicapa* (Spotted and African Dusky flycatchers).

SCRUB ROBINS
Family: Muscicapidae
Genus: *Cercotrichas* (Brown, Karoo, Kalahari, White-browed and Rufous-tailed scrub robins).

CHATS & WHEATEARS
Family: Muscicapidae
Genera: *Oenanthe* (Capped, Northern, Pied and Isabelline wheatears, and Buff-streaked Chat); *Cercomela* (Karoo, Tractrac, Sickle-winged and Familiar chats); *Saxicola* (African Stonechat and Whinchat).

WEAVERS
Family: Ploceidae
Genera: *Ploceus* (Chestnut, Village, Southern Brown-throated and Cape weavers, Lesser and Southern masked weavers, and Holub's and Eastern golden weavers); *Anaplectes* (Red-headed Weaver).

Kalahari Scrub Robin

BISHOPS & ALLIED SPECIES
Family: Ploceidae
Genera: *Quelea* (Red-billed, Red-headed and Cardinal queleas); *Euplectes* (Yellow-crowned, Southern Red, Black-winged and Yellow bishops, and White-winged, Red-collared, Fan-tailed, Long-tailed and Yellow-mantled widowbirds).

Family: Viduidae
Genera: *Vidua* (Pin-tailed and Shaft-tailed whydahs, Long-tailed and Broad-tailed paradise-whydahs, and Dusky, Purple, Twinspot and Village indigobirds); *Anomalospiza* (Cuckoo Finch).

SPARROWS
Family: Passeridae
Genera: *Passer* (House, Great and Cape sparrows, and Southern and Northern grey-headed sparrows); *Petronia* (Yellow-throated Petronia).

PIPITS & LONGCLAWS
Family: Motacillidae
Genera: *Anthus* (African, Mountain, Long-billed, Wood, Yellow-breasted, Plain-backed, Buffy, African Rock, Short-tailed, Bushveld, Striped, Tree and Red-throated pipits); *Macronyx* (Cape Longclaw); *Tmetothylacus* (Golden Pipit).

CANARIES & ALLIED SPECIES
Family: Fringillidae
Genera: *Crithagra* (Black-throated, Lemon-breasted, Yellow and White-throated canaries, Protea, Black-eared and Streaky-headed seedeaters, and Cape and Drakensberg siskins); *Serinus* (Black-headed Canary); *Emberiza* (Lark-like Bunting).

ILLUSTRATED GLOSSARY

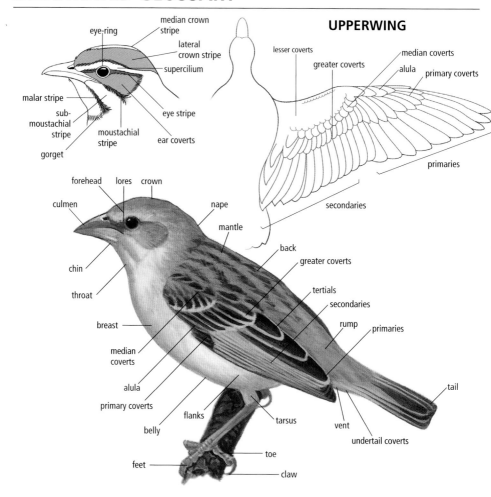

BIBLIOGRAPHY

Hockey, P, Dean, W & Ryan, P (eds). 2005. *Roberts' Birds of Southern Africa*. John Voelcker Bird Book Fund, Cape Town.

Liversidge, R. 'The African Pipit enigma' *Bulletin of the African Bird Club*, volume 5.2, September 1998.

Newman, K (revised by Newman, V). 2010. *Newman's Birds of Southern Africa*, Commemorative edition Struik Nature, Cape Town.

Sinclair, I, Hockey, P & Tarboton, W. 2002. *Sasol Birds of Southern Africa*, 3rd ed. Struik Nature, Cape Town.

Sinclair, I & Ryan, P. 2009. *Complete Photographic Field Guide – Birds of Southern Africa*. Struik Nature, Cape Town.

www.indigobirds.com
www.Xeno-canto.org
www.Macauleylibrary.com

INDEX